Ashraf's...

Tranc

Eye

A Series of Lectures & Aphorisms by
Contemporary Mashã'ikh & Islãmic Scholars

'Every religion has a distinguishing feature and, the salient feature of Islam is modesty (haya).' (Hadeeth)

Ashraf's Amãnat

An imprint of

Amãnah Studio

ଚ଼ର

*S*haykh-ul-Hadeeth Mawlana Muhammad Saleem Dhorat *hafizahullah* narrates,

'Life is time and time is life. Our age, our life, our times, our days, our nights, these valuable seconds, minutes and hours are all assets and commodities.

People view shares, dollars, cents, precious metals and diamonds all as commodities; similarly, time is an asset and commodity. Before spending pennies and pounds, shares and precious metals, a person questions whether it will bring profit or loss. A person will only spend if there is some tangible gain; if there is danger of loss, he will abstain. Moreover, if there is neither profit nor loss; a person will still abstain, why? Any activity or venture which does not bring profit is also a loss.

Accordingly, when we engage ourselves in viewing, listening or talking about futility we pacify ourselves by saying 'is it permissible or not?' Whereas the Sahābah ﷺ, Tābi'een ﷺ, Tabe Tābi'een ﷺ, our Aslāf ﷺ, they all self-assessed upon the principle and outlook, 'Will an activity benefit me in the Hereafter?'

By 'shopping' around one is able to achieve a ruling that listening or viewing live football, etc., etc., is permissible...but is it really beneficial and is it not harmful in the Hereafter? Ninety minutes of life are spent viewing futility; does it bring any profit either in this world or the Hereafter? If an activity does not bring loss, neither does it profit, then it is a loss, why? Because ninety minutes of your precious life has gone in waste to an activity that brought no gain, neither in this world nor the Hereafter.'

Ashraf's...

Tranquil Eye

Based Upon The Works

of

Shaykh Ashraf Ali Thãnwi ❁

Shaykh-ul-Hadeeth Muhammad Zakariyya Khandalvi ❁

Shaykh Mufti Mahmood Gangohi ❁

Shaykh Mufti Ahmad Khanpoori

Shaykh Mufti Muhammad Taqee Uthmani

Shaykh Mawlana Hakeem Muhammad Akhtar

Shaykh Mawlana Hashim ibn Hasan Jogwaree

Shaykh-ul-Hadeeth Mawlana Muhammad Saleem Dhorat

Series Editors

Mawlana Muhammad Maseehullah Patel

& Mawlana Qãri Yousuf

Prepared & Published

by

Mawlana Qãri Muhammad 'Abdullah Pg.Dip. LSJ

& Hãfiz Aslam Patel BA (Hons) Arch. Dip. Arch

Ashraf's Amãnat

An imprint of

Amãnah Studio

ൟ

Copyright Notice

Contents

Salāt & Salāms upon our Beloved Nabee ﷺ

Permission & Du'a

Shaykh Mufti

Mawlana Muhammad Taqee ibn Mufti Shafee' 'Uthmāni

Vice-President,
Darul Uloom Koranqi, Karachi

Assalamu Alaikum,

Editor,

Ashraf's Amānat

8th Zil Hijjah 1420

(14th March 2000)

$\mathcal{I}$ am pleased to give you permission for translating some of my discourses in *Islāhi Khutbaat*...If you undertake a new translation, you are permitted from my side.

May Allah ﷻ approve your efforts and make them beneficial for the Ummah.

Āmeen,

Was-salām,

(Shaykh Mufti)

Muhammad Taqee 'Uthmāni

Salāt & Salāms upon our Beloved Nabee ﷺ

Foreword

Shaykh-ul-Hadeeth

Mawlana Muhammad Saleem ibn Hafiz Ibraheem Dhorat

Principal Lecturer in Hadeeth, Jāmeah Riyādul-Uloom, Leicester

Islām is a code of life which encompasses every aspect of human existence. *Māshā'Allah*, my respected students Mawlana Maseehullah and Mawlana Muhammad 'Abdullah have reviewed this book on the subject of lustful gazing; the harms thereof and the comprehensive strategies outlined by contemporary Masha'ikh and Scholars for its prevention and cure.

It is only through the *Fadhl* of Allah ﷻ these publications have been granted wide acceptance and *Alhamdulillah* this very beneficial work has become available.

Readers will find herein fragrances of many flowers.

Nowadays, the subject of sex has been overexposed, degraded and misrepresented through channels of mass education and the media (especially on TV and Internet). Accordingly it is important to guide our youth in order to save them from sexual deviance.

May Allah ﷻ accept this work and make it a means of safeguarding the youth and a means of salvation in the Hereafter.

It is an honour for this humble one to be associated with Ashraf's Amānat.

What other Senior Scholars & Mashā'ikh have said about Ashraf's Amānat…

Shaykh 'Abdullah Kapodrawi of Canada…

'These publications contain the works of our pious predecessors & elders upon which we have full confidence. May Allah ﷻ grant greater barakah.'

Shaykh 'Abdul Hameed Isaac of South Africa…

'I am sure and, it is my du'aa, that by this great work Muslims living in western countries or whose mother tongue has become English, will be able to appreciate the great treasures of Islāmic Knowledge…'

Shaykh Mufti Rafee 'Uthmānee of Darul Uloom Korangi…

'Mashā'Allah! Excellent set of publications…'

Shaykh 'Abdur Ra'oof Lajpoori of UK…

'May Allah ﷻ grant ikhlaas and accept your services.'

Shaykh Ahmad Sadeeq Desai of South Africa…

'May Allah ﷻ accept your service & increase your Deeni activities.'

Shaykh Yusuf ibn 'Abdullah Darwan of UK…

'Through the infinite Mercy & Grace of Allah ﷻ, Ashraf's Amānat have published a series of beneficial Islāmic books. May Allah ﷻ grant them Tawfeeq to progress in this noble and rewarding endeavour and bless them with continuous ikhlaas & steadfastness…'

Shaykh Dr. Ismā'eel Mangera of South Africa…

'May Allah ﷻ fulfil your wishes to serve the Ummah. May your publications be a means of spreading the teachings of our akābir to others, young and old.'

Shaykh Mufti Zubayr Dudha of UK…

'May Allah ﷻ bless your endeavours.'

Shaykh Dr. Muhammad Sābir ﷺ…

'Shaykh Ashraf 'Ali Thānwi ﷺ narrated, 'After 50 years, my works will be translated and published on a large scale.' We are today witnessing this event…Mashā'Allah…the heart is pleased…this work is undoubtedly due to the sincerity of our cherished predecessors…'

Shaykh 'Abdur Rahmān Mangera of UK/USA…

'Bringing into English the spirit of the work of our pious predecessors is a very noble deed. May Allah ﷻ accept it.'

Shaykh Mufti Saiful Islam of UK…

'Alhamdulillah! The work being produced is very good…'

Shaykh Mufti Mahmood Dana of Barbados, West Indies…

'A beautiful selection of educational books…mainly based on the lectures, discourses & articles of great luminaries, scholars & achievers of Islām.'

Salāt & Salāms upon our beloved Nabee ﷺ

Introduction

Shaykh Mufti Muhammad Shafee ﷺ used to narrate,

> 'You blame society for our ill fortune, whereas you should mould your own surroundings. You should associate with such people who are adherents to the principals of the Sharee'ah, nobility and piety; those who forfeit such values have chosen a different path to you. Accordingly, create a network of like-minded associates and friends who help and aid in such matters and disassociate and shun those people who tread an altogether different path.'

The gift of tranquil vision, both external and spiritual, has been presented to the youth of the Muslim Ummah by the Final Messenger ﷺ of Allah ﷻ for two main reasons: protection of gaze and safeguarding of chastity and purity. Modesty, the distinguishing feature of Islam is being belittled by Muslim parents. We ourselves are to blame for this sad state of affairs (apparently the largest number of hits on unsavoury Internet websites emanate from Muslim countries/homes). If our elders were to return and view our behaviour and outlook they would undoubtedly reiterate the words of Allamah Iqbal ﷺ,

> 'They were surely your ancestors, but what are you? Sitting in idleness, waiting for tomorrow are you. Whose thinking is disgusted with ancestor's ways? No warmth is in the heart, no feelings in the soul. There is no respect for the message of Muhammad ﷺ in you. In fashion you are like the Ahl-e-Kitab, in culture you are like the Mushrik. Are these Muslims? Who put the Bani Isra'eel to embarrassment...'

Even the illiterate amongst our forefathers had certain noble characteristics and core values which the educated and technically enlightened of this era are unwilling to comprehend.

Immoral viewing of forbidden objects has become so widespread in Muslim homes and society that in most cases it is no longer considered impermissible (*harām*). In this regard, lewdness at home (TV and Internet), on the street, at places of study, work, shopping, advertising and upon on-line mediums has brought moral bankruptcy and frustration.

Prophet Muhammad ﷺ made the du'a, 'O Allah! Protect my chastity.' On another occasion he supplicated, 'O Allah! I seek you protection from the wickedness of my semen.' It appears in *hadeeth*, should one's gaze fall upon an outsider (*non-mahram*) and desires arise, then return to your spouse; for he or she undoubtedly possess the same faculty which other's possess. Prophet Muhammad ﷺ has also encouraged the early marriage of Muslim men and women in order to safeguard their gaze and chastity.

This brief book, inspired by the suggestions of Shaykh Yusuf ibn Qāri Muhammad Kara *hafizahullah* of Darul Uloom Bury and my Ustadh Shaykh-ul-Hadeeth Mawlana Yusuf Darwan *hafizahullah* of Darul Uloom Markaz/Darul Uloom Dawatul Imaan (West Yorkshire) is based predominantly upon the works of Contemporary Scholars. It is a humble attempt to highlight the causes, harms and cure for immoral gazing and misuse of the Internet and online forums. May Allah ﷻ accept the effort's of my Respected Father *hafizahullah* and make this kitab a means of our salvation.

(Mawlana) Maseehullah Patel

Darul Uloom Al-Amānah (Dewsbury & Darlaston)

Ramadhaan 1432 AH/August 2011 CE

Chapter One

Verses of the Glorious Qur'ān & Ahadeeth on Illicit Viewing

Shaykh Hashim ibn Hasan Jhogwari

hafizahullah

Reviewed by

Mawlana Qāri Yousuf Patel

Shaykh Ashraf Ali Thānwi ﷺ narrated, 'I have observed that from amongst a thousand maybe one person is saved from this illness; for it is a widespread malady.' *(Gadh al-Basr)*

قُل لِّلْمُؤْمِنِينَ يَغُضُّوا مِنْ أَبْصَارِهِمْ وَيَحْفَظُوا فُرُوجَهُمْ ذَلِكَ أَزْكَى لَهُـــمْ إِنَّ اللَّهَ خَبِيرٌ بِمَا يَصْنَعُونَ.

وَقُل لِّلْمُؤْمِنَاتِ يَغْضُضْنَ مِنْ أَبْصَارِهِنَّ وَيَحْفَظْنَ فُرُوجَهُنَّ وَلَا يُبْـــدِينَ زِينَتَهُنَّ إِلَّا مَا ظَهَرَ مِنْهَا وَلْيَضْرِبْنَ بِخُمُرِهِنَّ عَلَى جُيُوبِهِنَّ وَلَا يُبْـــدِينَ زِينَتَهُنَّ إِلَّا لِبُعُولَتِهِنَّ أَوْ آبَائِهِنَّ أَوْ آبَاءِ بُعُولَتِهِنَّ أَوْ أَبْنَـــائِهِنَّ أَوْ أَبْنَـــاءِ بُعُولَتِهِنَّ أَوْ إِخْوَانِهِنَّ أَوْ بَنِي إِخْوَانِهِنَّ أَوْ بَنِي أَخَوَاتِهِنَّ أَوْ نِسَائِهِنَّ أَوْ مَا مَلَكَتْ أَيْمَانُهُنَّ أَوِ التَّابِعِينَ غَيْرِ أُوْلِي الْإِرْبَةِ مِنَ الرِّجَالِ أَوِ الطِّفْلِ الَّذِينَ لَمْ يَظْهَرُوا عَلَى عَوْرَاتِ النِّسَاءِ وَلَا يَضْرِبْنَ بِأَرْجُلِهِنَّ لِيُعْلَمَ مَا يُخْفِينَ مِن زِينَتِهِنَّ وَتُوبُوا إِلَى اللَّهِ جَمِيعًا أَيُّهَ الْمُؤْمِنُونَ لَعَلَّكُمْ تُفْلِحُونَ.

'Tell the believing men that they must lower their gazes and guard their private parts; it is more decent for them. Surely Allah is All-Aware of what they do.

And tell the believing women that they must lower their gazes and guard their private parts, and must not expose their adornment, except that which appears thereof, and must wrap their bosoms with their shawls, and must not expose their adornment, except to their husbands or their fathers or the fathers of their husbands, or to their sons or the sons of their husbands, or to their brothers or the sons of their brothers or the sons of their sisters, or to their women, or to those owned by their right

*hands, or male attendants having no (sexual) urge, or to the
children who are not yet conscious of the shames of women. And
let them not stamp their feet in a way that the adornment they
conceal is known. And repent to Allah O believers, all of you, so
that you may achieve success.*

(*Súrah An-Núr, 24:30-31*)

haykh Maseehullah Khan ﷺ commented,
'*What do we take this Glorious Verse to imply? When
emerging outside to lower our gaze only when a handsome
person appears? We have restricted the ruling on immoral
gazing...however no restrictions are mentioned anywhere in this Verse.
Rather it is a general term applicable to viewing other people's
possessions, property, rank, business, residence, influence, standing, etc.,
etc. A common misconception is assuming this Verse to be only
applicable to viewing the beauty of an outsider. To view oneself with
arrogance and vanity is also immoral...to regard oneself as so-and-so, to
view with jealousy, greed, covetousness and conceit are all wrong...*'

(*Majalis Maseehul Ummat*)

haykh Mufti Muhammad Shafee' ﷺ writes in *Ma'ariful Qur'an*,
'*Súrah An-Núr contains many commands (ahkams) connected
to the protection of chastity and purity with stern prohibitions
upon immodesty and immorality. This Surah contains dire warnings
and outlines severe punishments for adultery and all avenues leading
unto it...because the Sharee'ah of Islam is a complete moderate way of life
it takes cognition of the natural urges and desires in humans and
outlines a permissible and pure avenue for their fulfilment. Furthermore,
in order to maintain human civilisation it was necessary to show a
wholesome method for man and woman to live and cohabit within
parameters; this is the institution of nikah (marriage) advocated by the
Glorious Qur'an and Sunnah.*'

With regards to this specific Verse,

> *'Ibn Katheer ⚇ has stated 'lowering of the gaze' implies that a Believer must turn away his gaze from all such visions which are classified as impermissible to view. This encompasses the prohibition of viewing a non-mahram person (without a valid Sharee' reason). This verse also prohibits the act of investigating the private lives, rooms, compounds and possessions of others.*

> **'...guard their private parts'**

> *This portion of the verse prohibits the fulfilment of desires through unlawful methods. This prohibition encompasses acts of voyeurism, fornication, homosexuality and masturbation...The purpose in this verse is to prohibit the fulfilment of desires via unlawful methods. To clarify this prohibition Allah ⚇ has stated the initial act which leads a person onto the path of fulfilling his/her desires (unnatural use of the gaze). This thereafter manifests in the fulfilling of desires, ultimately through fornication. Allah ⚇ mentions the initial and the ultimate whereby all that lies between (e.g. to touch and to talk etc.) also holds the same prohibition as the acts of ogling at non-mahram and fornication. '*

> *(ibid)*

A student wrote to Shaykh Ashraf 'Ali Thānwi ⚇, 'I am overwhelmed when beholding beauty and feel helpless to save my gaze from beautiful women.'

Hakeemul Ummat ⚇ replied, 'It is a principal of philosophy that will-power applies to acts of volition; accordingly if you have the power and urge to view beauties it follows you also have the power and choice not to view them. Whatever a person is able to do, he also has the choice of not doing. This is why Allah ⚇ mentions in the Glorious Qur'an:

> **'...Surely, the ear, the eye and the heart—each of them shall be interrogated about.'** *(17:35)*

Ahadeeth

*S*haykh Hashim ibn Hasan Jogwaree *hafizahullah* has related the following Ahadeeth in his kitab *Bad Nazree Ka Illaj*:

Accidental or Chance Glance

*S*ayyidduna Jareer ﷺ inquired from Rasoolullah ﷺ about the chance glance, wherein he replied, 'Immediately remove your gaze.'

(Muslim, Aboo Dawood, Tirmizi)

Benefits: Rasoolullah ﷺ has forbidden us to cast a second gaze after the first glance, meaning although the accidental or chance glance is forgiven and overlooked, any subsequent ogling or viewing is sinful.

Rights of the Road

*S*ayyidduna Abu Sa'eed al Khudree ﷺ related that Rasoolullah ﷺ narrated, 'Restrain yourself from sitting on the roads.' When people inquired, 'What if we have to out of necessity?' He ﷺ replied, 'In that case uphold the rights of the road.' 'What are they?' He ﷺ replied, 'They are to keep you gaze lowered; to not inconvenience another; to reply to the salam proffered; to promote good and forbid evil.' (Mishkāt)

Guarantee of Paradise

*S*ayyidduna 'Ubadah ibn Saamit ﷺ related that Rasoolullah ﷺ narrated, 'You become the guarantor of six items and I will become your guarantor of Jannah: When speaking do not lie; Do not break promises; Do not commit abuse of trust; Protect your private parts; Lower your gaze; Protect your hands from tyranny.' (Ahmad)

Gaze is a Poisonous Arrow of Shaytan

*S*ayyidduna 'Abdullah bin Mas'ood ◈ related that Rasoolullah ◈ narrated, 'The gaze is from amongst the poisonous arrows of Shaytan, whosoever refrains from it for the Sake of Allah, then Allah will grant him such sweetness and pleasure of Imaan which he will perceive in his heart.' (Tabranee)

Benefits: From amongst the tricks and deceptions Shaytan employs to deceive and mislead people, the gaze is a powerful and successful ploy. Firstly a person will observe and behold, thereafter thoughts and temptations (*wasawis*) arise, then he decides to enact and finally he becomes embroiled in sin. To save one self from adultery and to keep the gaze lowered are both necessary.

Protecting The Gaze & Pleasure in Worship

*S*ayyidduna Abu Umamah ◈ related that Rasoolullah ◈ narrated, 'Whosoever's gaze falls upon a beautiful women and he removes his gaze, then Allah ◈ will grant him in return such an act of worship whose pleasure he perceives in his heart.' (Tabranee)

Severe Warning upon Illicit Viewing

*S*ayyidduna Abu Umamah ◈ related that Rasoolullah ◈ narrated, 'Either you will keep your gaze lowered and protect your private parts or Allah ◈ will transfigure your faces.' (Tabranee)

Benefits: Rasoolullah ◈ has sounded an extremely severe warning in this Hadeeth whereas today this deed is regard as trivial, insignificant and not even a sin; mostly because whenever other sins are enacted a person tires from them sooner or later. In complete contrast, the more a person indulges in illicit viewing the stronger the urge to repeat becomes.

Cursed Man & Woman

Sayyidduna Hasan ؓ related that Rasoolullah ﷺ narrated, 'Allah ﷻ curses the ogling man and the ogled woman.'
(Mishkaat)

Curse implies distancing from mercy. The person who ogles and the person who encourages others to ogle by neglecting purdah and modesty are deprived of the Mercy of Allah ﷻ; what a misfortune and what deprivation.

Adulterous Eye

Rasoolullah ﷺ narrated, 'The eyes commit adultery and their fornication is to view (a non-mahram); the ears commit adultery and their fornication is to hear (non-mahram); the tongue too commits adultery and its fornication is to talk (to non-mahram); the hands too commit adultery and their fornication is to touch (a non-mahram).'

Modesty of Allah ﷻ

Rasoolullah ﷺ narrated, 'I am modest and Allah ﷻ is more modest than me and it is on account of modesty that Allah ﷻ has forbidden external and internal immorality.'   (Mishkaat)

Benefit: It is obvious this sin is extremely displeasing to Allah ﷻ; whoever enacts it causes Allah ﷻ to become abashed. The perpetrator is cursed, castigated and distanced from the Divine Court. Accordingly, whosoever claims affection for Allah ﷻ and His Rasool ﷺ should not raise his gaze towards non-mahram. When a person adopts taqwa, saves himself from external and internal sins, he acquires the Love and Proximity of Allah ﷻ...

The Eye Which Will Not Cry on Day of Judgement

Sayyidduna Aboo Hurayrah ◈ related that Rasoolullah ﷺ narrated, 'Every eye will cry on the Day of Judgement except the eye which refrained from viewing all those items decreed forbidden by Allah ﷻ; and the eye which stayed awake in the Path of Allah ﷻ; and the eye which cried because of the Fear of Allah ﷻ even though it may have been only a tear drop equal to the head of a fly.'   (Baihaqee)

Young Boys

Sayyidduna Aboo Hurayrah ◈ related that Rasoolullah ﷺ forbade a person to stare at a young boy. Sayyidduna Anas ◈ relates that Rasoolullah ﷺ narrated, 'Do not sit near young lads for their peril is greater than the danger from young ladies.'

Brother-in-Law

Rasoolullah ﷺ narrated, 'Save yourself from contact with non-mahram women.' Somebody inquired, 'What do you say regarding the brother-in-law?' Rasoolullah ﷺ replied, 'He is total death!'

Contact with one's brother-in-law is quite frequent therefore the chances of striking an illicit relationship is greater and more devastating, therefore he has been described as death.'

Chapter Two

Protecting
Gaze & Chastity

Shaykh Mufti Ahmad Khānpoori

damat barkātuhum

Grand Mufti, Darul Uloom Jamia Islāmia Dabhel, India

Reviewed

by

Mawlana Qāri Muhammad 'Abdullah

'Allamah Nawawee ❀ has described, 'Without a valid Sharee' reason, it is impermissible to view a non-mahram woman or young teenage boy.'

Necessity of Saving Oneself From Avenues of Sin

W hilst Islam has encouraged the acquisition of good habits and noble character, it has also stressed salvation from wickedness and bad behaviour: iniquity, lewdness and infidelity. All avenues leading unto adultery, such as lustful gazing, misappropriate use of the ears, hands and tongue, etc, have all been described as lewd behaviour (*fawàhish*). Although almost all worldly religions have prohibited adultery, however a salient and distinguishing feature of Islam is the strict prohibition and control of all those channels, means and avenues leading unto infidelity.

For example, where Islam has forbidden the consumption of alcohol, it has not stopped at only making drinking of alcohol impermissible. Rather to reinforce the prohibition it has ruled on so many avenues associated with alcohol. For example, the manufacturing, transporting, handling, selling and serving of alcohol are all forbidden; just as the drinking of alcohol is impermissible.

Another example is the prohibition of idol worship; all avenues leading unto it, for example, model making, drawing and photography of animate objects all have been prohibited. Similarly all channels leading unto this impermissible act have also been forbidden. People used to worship the sun at fixed times; accordingly even performance of salāh at sun-rise, zenith (noon) and sun-set have been prohibited for Muslims to dispel any notion to an onlooker of sun worship; whereas the performer of salāh is not worshipping the sun. Nevertheless even the remotest semblance has been removed.

Worldly Example

This concept is easily understood form the national protection programs which frequently take place at times of feared pandemics. A massive campaign and operation is swung into operation. For example, if there is threat of Malaria spreading, Governments and NGO's will embark not only on a campaign of immunisation but also of education and prevention. Various media outlets will be used to inform the public of the dangers; method of infection and preventative measure. High graphic boards will show the various types of mosquito's, their breeding habits, likely locations and the measures to be adopted to prevent them from entering communal and living areas. For example, covering and disinfecting of drains and open-sewers; avoiding ponds, canals and stagnant waters in rainy seasons; allowing daylight to penetrate and air rooms; using mosquito net impregnated with an insecticide over your bed and spraying and vaporising rooms at dusk and during the night with an insecticide; after sunset, wearing long sleeves, trousers and socks - ankles are a particular target for mosquito's; applying an insect repellent to your skin and clothes; covering bedroom doors and windows with fine mesh netting, etc, etc.

Observe, how all avenues of disease transmission are being addressed systematically and thoroughly, only then is there a fair chance of being saved from this disease.

Similarly, Islam has adopted the same approach in order to stop the possibility of sins and evil. Where sins have been prohibited; so have avenues leading unto it.

Restrictions On Avenues of Adultery

Adultery is a deadly disease and an extremely grave sin about which the Glorious Quran warns, 'Do not even go near to adultery.' Islam has restricted all avenues which lead unto adultery; for example the intermingling of non-mahram men and women; the emergence of Muslim ladies without purdah to the extent they have been instructed to remain firmly within their residences. When a genuine need does arise to emerge, for which the Sharee'ah has stipulated conditions, then it is permissible. Without these pre-conditions or genuine need it is not permissible.

When the need arises, the donning of burqa, within the spirit of purdah, concealing one's beauty and personality; to the extent wearing of noisy trinkets and jewellery is banned. Why? The sound of jewellery is enough to instigate desires in a person. Similarly, the wearing of perfume is forbidden; it appears in hadeeth, 'A woman who emerges outside wearing perfume and passes by men is an adulteress.' (*Tirmizee*)

Men are instructed, whenever a genuine need arises to communicate with a non-mahram woman, then this should be from behind a screen; she should not be viewed; protect your vision; lower your gaze; protect your modesty; all these instructions to prevent the ultimate act of adultery. Amongst the fundamentals of Deen is this prohibition upon all avenues which lead unto sin.

Modesty is a Fundamental Teaching of Prophet Muhammad ﷺ

Simultaneous to this exclusion on adultery, hedonism and profligacy is an even greater emphasis on modesty, restraint and chastity, which forms a fundamental feature of the teachings of Rasoolullah ﷺ.

It appears in Bukhãree Shareef, when Rasoolullah ﷺ sent a letter of invitation towards Islam to the Roman Emperor Heraclius Augustus

(574–641 CE); the latter had travelled to Bayt-ul-Maqdis (Jerusalem) to fulfil a vow. The letter was delivered here via a Syrian Governor. Upon receiving the letter, Heraclius sought to find information on the sender; for he himself was an accomplished scholar (ranked second only to the Pope) of the Christian faith and aware of the signs predicted of the Final Prophet. Heraclius addressed his advisors, 'Make inquiries about the sender, see if you are able to meet anybody from his locality.' The advisors suggested, 'People from Arabia regularly come to Shām for trade; we should be able to locate somebody.' Coincidentally, a caravan led by Aboo Sufyan ibn Harb (560-650 CE), who had not accepted Islam at the time and was synonymous as leader of those *Quraysh* who harboured enmity towards Muslims, had just arrived. He, together with his associates was summoned and quizzed.

Amongst questions, the final one relevant to this study was when Heraclius asked, 'What does this Prophet command you to do?' Aboo Sufyan replied, 'He commands us to worship Allah, the only god and no one else; to not associate anybody besides Him...this Prophet also gives us four directives; salāh, honesty, chastity (*'iffat*) and cordiality with relatives (*silah rahmee*).' (*Bukhāree*)

In a nutshell, even an antagonist, at the time, of the calibre of Aboo Sufyan testified to the basic value of modesty advocated by Prophet Muhammad ﷺ to one of his arch rivals.

Chastity (*'iffat*) - the lesson from Surah Yousuf

'Iffat means to protect oneself from immorality, immodesty and adultery. *'Iffat* is the condition praised and ordained by the Glorious Quran, reflected especially in the episode of Prophet Yousuf ﷺ. Whatever episodes are related in the Glorious Quran are for a specific reason; to emphasise to the reader an explicit lesson and message.

Your Ladies Too Will Remain Chaste

Prophet Muhammad ﷺ was a great advocator of chastity; in a narration he relates, 'You adopt chastity and your ladies will remain chaste.' If a person wishes the womenfolk of his family remain faithful and pure, he should adopt these same values and moral principals for himself. Similarly, if you treat your parents with respect and esteem, then your children will treat you with reverence.

Fate Does Not Favour

Allah ﷻ has established certain values, order and a sense of justice in this universe,

> *'Herewith from the dome resounds;*
>
> *'Whatever is sounded rebounds.''*

In this world we reap what we sow, Divine Fate does not take anybody into consideration in such matters. One's lineage, rank, post, wealth or standing; whosoever operates beyond these core values will be apprehended. 'You adopt chastity and your ladies will remain chaste.' It is evident from this if there are any shortcomings in our behaviour the disastrous repercussions will be felt by the womenfolk of our household. Numerous incidents testify to this principal.

A Heart Rendering Episode

An associate informed me of how a qualified academic was given the opportunity to undertake Deeni service in a locality. Here he became entangled with a young woman to the extent they reached an adulterous union. Such events very rarely remain unhidden; accordingly people began to gossip. When elders of the community became aware of this unsavoury development, they acted sympathetically; 'he is a young unmarried man; we should wed and alleviate him from this predicament.' They refrained from acting rashly and gave him an opportunity to reform; acting with wisdom and compassion. This was the way of our elders and also the path chosen by our Creator. Even today, civilised nations allow citizens an opportunity to make amends.

Accordingly the elders encouraged a noble pious and beautiful young lady to marry this academic. However, his temperament had become corrupted, 'a person who becomes infatuated with junk food finds wholesome home cooking boring.' Even with a beautiful young wife at home he was still infatuated in the previous relationship. When the elders saw how he was pushing his wife out and sleeping with the lewd woman, they intervened and took a stand.

He was thrown out of the community; however events transpired later on in life, when his wife became entangled in an adulterous union; in old-age he had to suffer the ignominy of being thrown out of his own house and observing his wife now indulging in adultery with another man. His death also arrived in this state of disgrace.

Another Example

If you adopt chastity and modesty, your womenfolk will remain pure and chaste. This is one example of Divine Retribution and Justice. Another example, which has also been related by Shaykh Zulfiqar Naqhshabandi *damat barakatuhum*.

There was a goldsmith whose wife was very beautiful and of good character. One day when he returned from his shop he noticed her weeping profusely. He asked, 'What is the matter?' 'She replied, 'This servant of ours, whom we have raised since he was a child, has turned out to be so treacherous that when he returned home with some vegetables, he grabbed my hand with what I sensed as passion in his heart. Such disloyalty and unfaithfulness.' Hearing this tears welled in the goldsmiths' eyes and he too began to sob. 'Why are you crying?' his wife asked. The goldsmith replied, 'This is a punishment for my misbehaviour, today a lady came to buy some bracelets. She asked me to put them on for her; I found her hands very attractive and pressed them with passion. This is the result. 'You reap what you sow.' *(Kasful Khifa)* This is why Rasoolullah ﷺ narrated,

> *'You remain chaste and your womenfolk will remain virtuous and endeavour to protect themselves from sins.'*

Repercussion of Parental Disobedience

Another example of this Divine Retribution is behaviour with parents. If you behave with decorum and kindness with them; your children and juniors will reciprocate this. Qadhi Abu 'Ali Tanukhi ﷺ narrates in his kitab *Nishwarul Muhadhirath*, 'A child lassoed a rope around his father's feet and thereafter dragged him outside the house. When they reached a specific place, only then did the father speak, 'Son, enough! Do not drag me any further!' 'Why?' inquired his son. 'I too had tied a rope around my father's feet and it was to this point that I had hauled him, today you are enacting the very same behaviour with me.'

Shaykh Arshad Madanee *damat barakatuhum* relates how a sweet seller in Delhi witnessed a neighbour across the street throw his father from the balcony of their shop into the gutter where he later died. Now this person only had daughters and the sweet seller relates, 'I had heard from 'Ulama and Mashā'ikh that a person's behaviour and attitude towards his parents is replicated by his own children; yet this neighbour of mine only has daughters and I have witnessed him act unjustly and cruelly with his father; how will he fare?' One day, many years later, whilst sitting in the shop I witnessed one of my neighbour's daughters dressed in burqa arrive and throw him over the balcony in the same despicable manner he had thrown his father so many years previously.'

The Compassion of Rasoolullah ﷺ with a Young Person

Once a young man visited Rasoolullah ﷺ and requested, 'O Rasool of Allah! Grant me permission to fornicate?' Observe the kindness and affection of Rasoolullah ﷺ, for if somebody were to come to us and speak in this manner, we would belittle, scold and rebuke. Rasoolullah ﷺ seated him down and explained, 'Tell me, this act of fornication which you are proposing will be with some woman?' The young man replied, 'Yes.' Rasoolullah ﷺ commented, 'If somebody were to perform such an act with your sister, will you find it acceptable?' 'No, never,' the young man replied. Rasoolullah ﷺ commented, 'If somebody were to act in this manner with your mother, will you find it acceptable?' 'No, never,' the young man replied. Rasoolullah ﷺ commented, 'With your maternal aunt?' 'No, never,' the young man replied. Rasoolullah ﷺ commented, 'With your paternal aunt?' 'No, never,' the young man replied. Rasoolullah ﷺ commented, 'The person with whom you wish to act in this manner will undoubtedly be somebody's sister, mother, maternal aunt or paternal aunt.' Immediately he replied, 'I will not act in this manner.' Thereafter, Rasoolullah ﷺ placed his blessed hand upon the young man's chest and supplicated, 'O Allah! Remove the dirt and filth from his heart.' The Sahābee ؓ who related this episode commented, 'Henceforth this young man's gaze always remained lowered.' This was the blessing of Rasoolullah's ﷺ du'a.

Deprivation from Sexual Pleasure

Rasoolullah ﷺ also commented, 'Do not initiate adultery for you will be deprived from the pleasures of love making with your wife. You adopt chastity and your women will remain chaste. So-and-so community indulged in adultery; consequently their women too became adulteresses.' *(Kasful Khifa)*

Allah ﷻ Forgave Kifl

An episode is related in Tirmizee Shareef of how Rasoolullah ﷺ described the fate of a person from a previous Ummah. 'Abdullah bin 'Umar ؓ, the narrator relates, 'This episode I have heard from Rasoolullah ﷺ not once, not twice, not thrice, not seven times but even more...' This highlights how Rasoolullah ﷺ would repeatedly relate advises which he considered imperative for his Companions and Ummah. We are loathed to related such incidents more than once for fear of being labelled boring or lacking in knowledge.

There was a person amongst the Banu Isra'eel by the name of Kifl. A lady came to him and pleaded, 'My children are starving, please be of assistance to us.' Kifl gave her seven dinars on the condition she would let him fornicate with her. She took the money for her children and thereafter presented herself, however, she began to shiver and shake violently. Observing this vicious trembling, Kifl spoke, 'I have neither forced or committed any violence upon you; who have arrived voluntarily and of your free will, so why this condition?' The lady replied, 'I have never committed such a treacherous act before in my life, my children's predicament has brought me here, this is why my body is not willing.' She began to sob uncontrollably. Noticing this heart -rendering scene, Kifl too became remorseful upon his lifestyle, he immediately repented and gifted the seven dinars he had given her.

Kifl passed away that very night. Allah's ﷻ relationship with the Banu Isra'eel meant any deed they undertook would be recorded on their door threshold the next morning. Similarly, when any amongst them repented, and his repentance was accepted, this too would be recorded. Now people were unaware of the previous night's developments, they all assumed Kifl to be a wicked person. In the morning, they found written on his threshold, 'Allah ﷻ has forgiven Kifl.'

Prophetic Quality

To save oneself from sin is a quality beloved to Allah ﷻ, especially on those occasions when the means and opportunity to sin are present.

Imam Ghazāli ﷫ has related in *Ihya-ul-Uloom* the episode of a Tabi'ee Sulaiman bin Yassar ؓ (d. 105 AH), an extremely knowledgeable and handsome Scholar who lived in Madeenah Munawwarah and who during his childhood served *Umm–ul-Mumineen* Maimoonah ؓ and Aishah ؓ. Once he departed for Makkah Mukarramah with a companion for Hajj. Along route, they camped at Abwa. His companion went to the local village to purchase provisions. Where they had camped was overlooked by a hill, upon which were Bedouin houses. From here emerged an extremely beautiful woman, who upon observing Sulaiman bin Yassar ؓ below became infatuated with him and came down to seduce him. She removed her niqab and appeared as resplendent as the full moon. As she spoke, Sulaiman bin Yassar ؓ mistook her to be a beggar asking for food; and as he hurried to find something for her, she spoke, 'I am not in need of food, but seek from you what a woman seeks from a man!'

Sulaiman bin Yassar ؓ replied, 'Shaytan has sent you here.' He then placed his head between his knees and began to cry profusely. Afraid at being apprehended or disgraced, the Bedouin women left hurriedly.

Sulaiman's ؓ companion now returned from the village and as he entered noticed Sulaiman's ؓ face and eyes reddened. He inquired, 'What is the matter?' 'Nothing, I remembered my wife and children.' 'No, it is something else, your condition testifies to it?' Upon his companions insistence, Sulaiman ؓ related what had happened. Hearing this episode, his companion began to cry. Sulaiman ؓ inquired, 'Brother, why do you cry?' He replied, 'It is Allah's grace and favour that I was not in your position for I would undoubtedly have become submerged in sin under such circumstance. I cry out of gratefulness to Allah ﷻ.'

Thereafter they proceeded for Hajj, arrived in Makkah Mukarramah, performed *tawaaf* and sat down in meditation between Maqaam Ibraaheem and Hajr-Aswad. Due to tiredness, he fell into slumber and observed in a dream Sayyiduna Yousuf ﷺ; extremely handsome and young. Sulaiman ؈ asked him, 'Who are you?' 'I am Yousuf.' Sulaiman ؈ inquired, 'Yousuf the Siddeeq (truthful)?' 'Yes.' Sulaiman ؈ commented, 'Your episode with Zulaikah is truly amazing!' Sayyiduna Yousuf ﷺ replied, 'Your episode with the Bedouin women from Abwa is even more amazing.'

Two More Amazing Episodes

'Allamah Yafa'ee ؈ mentions in his kitab *At Targheeb wat Tarheeb*, 'Events and episodes occur in a person's life where his or her chastity and modesty are tested. When such events take place, some people who had relished and awaited such opportunities become embroiled in sin. However, there are also some courageous servants of Allah ﷻ, who when confronted by such events choose to save themselves. They are then honoured and elevated...

There was a young man, whose body and clothes always radiated with the fragrance of musk and amber. An acquaintance commented, 'You are an amazing fellow, spending such large amounts on top quality fragrances, every time we meet, some aroma radiates from you.' The young man replied, 'By Oath of Allah ﷻ! I have not spent a penny on fragrance.' 'Then where does this scent come from?' 'That is a secret which I do not wish to divulge.' 'No you must tell me.'

'Man yearns what is prohibited unto him.'

It is a trait of man to hanker after something which is prohibited.

Accordingly, this friend insisted upon his secret, whereupon the young man related. 'I worked in my father's household store. One day an old lady purchased a lot of goods and requested my father to instruct me to carry them to her home and collect payment. I left with her and arrived at her residence, which was a huge mansion. We entered a grand living room, wherein a young beautiful woman was sitting upon a couch. Upon observing me, she came across, grabbed my hand and began pulling me towards the couch. Agitated and perplexed, I tried to move away, but she kept pulling and seducing me. The only ploy that came to my mind was to make an excuse to visit the lavatory. She instructed her servants to clean the en-suite toilet before I entered. I relieved my self and took my own faeces and splattered it all over my clothes and body to make myself appear reprehensible and unappealing. As soon as I reappeared she flew into a rage and shouted to her maid-servants to return this 'mad man to the bedlam!'

I had one dirham in my pocket with which I purchased some soap and lowered myself into the river to clean my clothes and body as best as possible. That night when I retired to bed, I observed an Angel in human form in a dream, he spoke, 'I have been sent by Allah 🕮 to give you glad tidings of Paradise in lieu of your saviour from sin.' He thereafter applied some fragrance to my clothes, body and spoke, 'In the way you applied faeces to protect your self from sin, you are being rewarded.' From that morning unto this day, the aroma and scent remains with me.'

'Allamah Yafa'ee 🕮 mentions another episode. 'A young wealthy man was squandering his time and wealth in high-living and hedonism. Coincidentally, a young widow in the neighbourhood, whose children had not eaten anything for three days borrowed her friend's clothes to venture outside to seek assistance. As she walked passed the residence of this young man, he took a fancy and summoned her over and proposed to sleep with her. Instantly the young widow began to cry and spoke, 'When you summoned me, I thought you were going to show an act of kindness and generosity towards me and my children who have not eaten for three days; I am not the type of woman who indulges in fornication! I have come out of my house to seek assistance for my children not to indulge in harlotry!'

Humiliated and ashamed, the wealthy young man gifted some money to her with dignity and thereafter reflecting upon his sinful existence to date, repented for his transgressions.

He had a habit of recording his daily activities in a diary. When he returned to his mother that night he mentioned this incident to her, who being aware of his profligacy expressed her delight at this act of kindness and suggested he write this act of goodness in his diary as well. 'There is no space in my diary; it is full of sins,' replied the young man. His mother insisted, 'Write it in the margins or footnote.' Accordingly, he wrote it down and retired to sleep a remorseful and heart-broken person.

When he awoke for Fajr Salāh the next morning, he noticed the whole diary pristine white and blank...except for the one incident of kindness of the previous day which was written in the margin. Underneath was written the Qur'ānic Verse,

> '*Establish Salāh at both ends of the day, and in the early hours of night. Surely, good deeds erase bad deeds. That is a reminder for the mindful.*' (*Glorious Qur'ān, 11:114*)

In Islam '*iffat* and modesty are treasured and valued qualities. In the early epoch of Islam, when the Companions (Sahābah ﷺ) spread throughout the world in their mission to propagate Islam, enemies would use the ploy of lining their young beautiful maidens en-route in an attempt to distract and deviate these Companions; however because they had enjoyed the company of Rasoolullah ﷺ; he had trained them to keep their gazes lowered and protect their chastity. This lowering of the gaze is paramount in protecting oneself from adultery.

Mahram & Non-Mahram Ladies

There are two classes of ladies: *mahram* and *non-mahram*. *Mahram* are those with whom marriage (nikah) at anytime in life is not possible. For example, mother, sisters, grandmothers, maternal and paternal aunts, nieces, granddaughters, etc. All these are known as *mahram* and purdah from them is not necessary because nikah with them will always be impermissible (*haram*).

Those ladies with whom it may be possible, sometime in life, to get married to are known as *non-mahram*. It does not matter if they are currently married to another male; but the moment their nikah breaks, whether through divorce or death of their husband, then immediately after the period in waiting (*iddat*), it would be possible to perform nikah with them, then all such ladies are known as *non-mahram*. It is not permissible (*halāl*) to view such ladies without a valid Sharee' reason.

In our society, despite some ladies being categorised as *non-mahram*, because of family relationships they are incorrectly assumed to be *mahram*. For example, aunties married to paternal or maternal uncles, they are only haram as long as they are in the nikah of one's uncle; should the latter divorce her or pass away and her *iddat* finishes it would be permissible to marry her; therefore she is a *non-mahram*.

Similarly, our society wrongly considers paternal and maternal cousins also as *mahram* whereas they are not in the same class as one's sister's; nikah with cousins is permissible. Therefore it is necessary to adopt purdah with them, in fact it is more important because one comes into greater contact with cousins.

Absent Husbands

Rasoolullah ﷺ narrated,

> *'Do not visit those women whose husband's are absent or on journeys.'* *(Mishkaat)*

When a spouse is absent, sometimes there is a tendency for weak individuals to feel unfettered and attracted towards others. When a *non-mahram* visits such a person in solitude, then desires and the urge to sin are instigated by one's own self (nafs) and Shaytan because the means to misbehave are greater and restrictions and prohibitions fewer.

This is why somebody queried, 'O Rasoolullah ﷺ! What do you say of the brother-in-law?' Rasoolullah ﷺ replied, 'The brother-in-law is death!' Just as a person endeavours to distance himself from death so should a person distance and caution oneself from a brother or sister-in-law; for the chances of misbehaviour with them is greater due to regular family interaction which on many occasions go unnoticed for a long time. Relates Akbar Illabaadi ﷺ (1846-1921 CE),

> *'The consequence of non-purdah is skew;*
>
> *he who was considered son turned out to be the nephew.'*

The Sharee'ah has stipulated purdah; control your gaze and protect your vision from *non-mahram*. The first Qur'ānic Verse is directed at men,

> *'Tell the believing men they must lower their gazes and guard their private parts; it is more decent for them. Surely Allah is All-Aware of what they do.'* *(24:30)*

The following verse is directed at ladies,

'And tell the believing women they must lower their gazes and guard their private parts, and must not expose their adornment...' (24:31)

In the Glorious Qur'an, whenever a Command is stipulated then all believers are addressed generally, for example, 'O Believers!' herein both genders are included, however this one command is of such a nature wherein both men and women are uniquely addressed separately in order to emphasise the importance of this teaching.

Ogling Destroys Effulgence (Nur) of the Face

Rasoolullah ﷺ narrated,

'Keep your gazes lowered and protect your chastity otherwise Allah ﷻ will destroy the effulgence (nur) from your faces.'

(Al Targheeb)

When an eclipse takes place, sunlight is overshadowed by the darkness of the moon, similarly when a person indulges in surreptitious ogling, then no matter how handsome he or she may be, their face loses vivacity and effulgence.

Today it has become extremely difficult to control one's gaze, firstly because it is a pandemic habit; secondly due to widespread nudity and immorality. Men and women stroll the streets in inappropriate and immodest attire; images are beamed all around us; nevertheless those who wish to acquire the Pleasure of Allah ﷻ; the Affection and Love of Allah ﷻ; the reformation of one's self; the special Bond and Proximity to Allah ﷻ in their hearts; then they will have to save themselves from this sinful habit.

All the *Mashā'ikh* are unanimous that reformation of the heart is not possible with ogling and staring; whereas there are greater sins, nevertheless the ramification of this particular sin is so severe as to prohibit any hope of reformation. Shaykh-ul-Hadeeth Zakariyya ﷺ has written in *Aap Beeti*, 'Many are the *Zākireen* who try to acquire *nur* in their hearts through *dhikr*, however on account of immoral gazing they are deprived.'

Why Is Pleasure From Worship Not Achieved?

Nowadays although we perform salāh, recite the Glorious Qur'ān, make *thikr* and adopt a life of some precaution, nevertheless we fail to derive pleasure from these acts of worship and abstinence, why? One major reason is immoral gazing. It is a dangerous habit which is difficult to remove once accustomed to because it requires very little in terms of means. For example, a person involved in adultery has to adopt certain measures; they need a willing accomplice, time, opportunity, strength and place. Whereas immoral gazing according to Shaykh Ashraf 'Ali Thānwi ﷺ is such an endemic disease that even when half the body is dangling in the grave (i.e. old-age), it still does not weaken. Even many pensioners are voyeurs, not in the least remorseful nor considering it to be wrong. If congregated somewhere and a mother and daughter were to pass, they willingly ogle at both, for the sin is so secretly carried out nobody else becomes aware. Shaykh, Mawlana, Qari, Hafiz, Chairman, President, Secretary, Father, Uncle and Grandfather all retain their titles and rank even when submerged in this sin, because nobody else is aware.

Organs & Faculties Are A Trust (Amanah)

Allah ﷺ says in the Glorious Qur'ān:

> '...*Undoubtedly, the ears, eyes and heart, of each of them one shall be interrogated.*' (17:36)

Allah ﷺ created us and bestowed us with various faculties: eyes to view; ears to hear; tongue to taste and speak; hands to touch; feet to support and walk; mind to contemplate and ponder; skeleton to support; skin to house the internal organs and protect us from the elements; numerous parts of the body perfectly organised and working in tandem; a trust from Allah ﷻ gifted and loaned to us for a pre-determined limited time to be used accordingly. It is a borrowed entity to be taken away and questioned about. We are obliged to employ it in accordance to the guidance offered by it's Creator; within confines of those avenues decreed by Him.

Why is Lustful Gazing Prohibited?

The eye is a great bounty (*nemat*) from Allah ﷻ, consider it to be a camera through which different images enter and are then processed by the mind and stored in memory. All these images viewed by the eye cause a reaction. If you were to view the Holy Kabah (*Kabatullah*); at the moment of viewing, the Splendour, Glory and Love of Allah ﷻ arises; such affection which is indescribable and produces a state of longing for this experience to remain forever.

When we view our parents, elders, ustadh and pious (*Ahlullah*) the state of our mind is totally different; all because of the images being conveyed upon our hearts by those whom we consider our seniors.

When we view the ill, needy, destitute, those undergoing some form of hardship; when such images reach our mind and hearts, instinctively mercy, compassion, sympathy and an urge to help and be of benefit in some form or another arises.

Whenever we view oppression, tyranny, injustice, assault or wrong being committed to another person, instantly a sense of fair play and natural justice arises. The drive to intervene, be merciful (*rahm*) and to aid the wronged party takes hold; simultaneously the urge to detest (*tanaffur*) the guilty party arises in our temperament.

The aim of this elaboration is to display the correlation between viewing and the emotions, feelings and desires which consequently arise. Similarly, the viewing of a strange woman, a beautiful woman, a beautiful figure all instigate desires and longing to commit acts which entail the disobedience of Allah ﷻ. It is this vision, this eyesight which acts as the medium through which images and signals are relayed to the heart and mind and which trigger a series of emotional reactions. This is why the Sharee'ah has outlined commands which seek to control this reaction, we are allowed to view permissible objects and items but are also prohibited to view impermissible substance.

Vision - An Amazing Bounty (Nemat)

The eye is such an amazing bounty gifted by Allah ﷻ which is only truly appreciated by the one who does not have it. Shaykh Mufti Muhammad Taqee Uthmani *hafizahullah* narrates, 'Scientists have formulated that in coming from darkness into light and vice-versa, the fibres of the eyes contract and expand up to a distance of nine miles in an instance.' This is the power, might and supremacy of Allah ﷻ, and upon His Creation has Allah ﷻ outlined promises and warnings to us.

Virtues of Spouses Viewing Each Other

It appears in Hadeeth when any of the spouses view each other with affection then Allah ﷻ looks upon both of them with His Gaze of Mercy. The gaze of love and desire is not being prohibited completely, it is being channelled in halal avenues; look where you are permitted and encouraged to view; not everybody. Nowadays, our behaviour is totally opposite; we look with contempt upon our spouse yet ogle and stare with lust, mercy, love and longing upon a *non-mahram*.

Similarly, it appears in Hadeeth, an obedient pious child is able to attain the reward of an accepted Hajj and Umrah merely by gazing with mercy and affection upon his parents. The Companions inquired, 'O Rasoolullah ﷺ! What if a person views his parents in this manner a hundred times a day?' Rasoolullah ﷺ replied, 'Allah ﷻ is great and pure. If you view a hundred times a day, you will acquire reward of a hundred Hajj and Umrah.' There is no need to undertake the arduous journey and expense of (*nafl*) Hajj and Umrah when one is able to acquire the same reward by sitting at home.

Analogy of Harms of Lustful Gazing

In discussing the various repercussions of viewing and their resultant commands, one should consider the analogy of a person who has suffered a heart attack and is in bed in hospital. When visitors arrive, the doctor will have guided his nursing staff to ensure nobody brings tales of woe, tears or sorrow lest his weakened heart takes effect and suffers further bouts of pain. Antagonists, emotional weaklings and idiots are also prohibited from visiting for fear of upsetting his weak physique and heart.

Similarly, those matters which are harmful unto you, your deen and Imaan, all have been prohibited. This is precisely why the viewing of *non-mahram* women and young men has been prohibited.

Greatest Trial & Turmoil (*fitnah*)

Generally, one of the greatest trials or temptations (*fitnah*) which Shaytan employs in this world is the misuse of lewd women as a trap. It appears in Bukhāree Shareef,

> *'After me I have not witnessed for men a greater trial (fitnah) than women.'*

Men of great intellect have had their senses snatched away by women. Once Rasoolullah ﷺ addressed a gathering of women,

'From a Deeni and intellectual perspective I have not seen a more imperfect person than you who could rob the intellect, experience and understanding of a man.' (Bukhāree)

Although Allah ﷻ has granted us vision, we are not allowed unrestricted viewing. This is why we have been prohibited to view *non-mahram*.

What Difference & Repercussion?

Shaykh Ashraf 'Ali Thānwi ﷺ narrated, 'Some people consider the viewing of a beautiful face as the same as viewing a beautiful building. However, this is not true, there is a big difference.' It appears in Hadeeth,

'Whosoever views the beauty of a woman, then on Day of Judgement, molten lead will be poured into his eyes.' (Nasbul Raya)

If a speck of dust, grit or water enters our eyes, we become agitated and perturbed. What then of molten lead? This is why it is beneficial to ponder upon the warnings sounded for lustful gazing, this makes prevention much easier. In another Hadeeth it appears,

'The lustful gaze is an arrow from the arrows of Shaytan. Whosoever, on account of My Fear forgoes it, I shall transform it into such sweetness which he will experience in his heart.' (Tabrānee)

'Allamah Ibn Qayyum ﷺ comments, 'When a person views *non-mahram* women, then before his gaze is able to affect others it harms him. It is such a weapon which harms the instigator first.'

Thereafter, Rasoolullah ﷺ presents a beautiful promise from Allah ﷻ, '...Whosoever, on account of My Fear forgoes it, I shall transform it into such sweetness which he will experience in his heart.' If we desire this sweetness we shall have to undertake some opposition (*mujahadah*).

Deprivation From Pleasure of Worship

This is why Mashā'ikh have stated the person involved in lustful gazing is deprived from sweetness of the heart and the pleasure of worship. There are many other sins, however those have not had the same warning and repercussions outlined as for this one. Shaykh Ashraf Ali Thānwi ۞ narrated, 'People consider this sin as ever so light as to regard it insignificant even after committing it. Moreover, other sins, after repeated involvement produces lethargy. For example, a person who consumes alcohol; drinks one bottle, two bottles, three bottles, sooner or later he tires and stops due to physical incapacity. Similarly, a person involves himself in adultery, but for how long? Until his body is able to cope, sooner or later his legs will give way. Such is the outcome with every sin except lustful gazing which has no ending!

A person will ogle for one hour, two hours, three hours and-on-and-on; acquiring what he considers to be lust in his arrogance and stupidity; however understand this to be no yearning; it is fire, the flames of which are deceiving and smouldering within the heart. They will forever sparkle and flicker whenever you stand for salāh or any other activity, they will keep reappearing and contort your life and existence.'

A person once wrote, 'Shaykh, although I have control over focussing my gaze I do not have the strength to remove my gaze.' Shaykh Ashraf 'Ali Thānwi ۞ replied, 'Despite being so educated and learned in philosophy, you are talking in this manner? Control applies to matters over which one has choice, whether to enact or not...when you have the power to focus your gaze, then of a surety you have the power to remove your gaze.' Another letter arrived, 'When I save my gaze, a great pain is felt by the heart; regret and sorrow arises, 'Wow, what beauty she must possess, what eyes, nose, etc...a wound is felt by the heart.'

Shaykh Ashraf 'Ali Thānwi ﷺ answered by posing a question, 'Tell me, in not ogling how long does the heart feel agitated and for how long is the heart perturbed when you do view non-mahram?'

The person replied, 'When I do not ogle, the regret is felt for a few minutes and thereafter sweetness is experienced; but when I do look, for three days and nights I imagine her features and my heart remains in turmoil.'

Shaykh Ashraf 'Ali Thānwi ﷺ answered, 'You yourself should conclude whether it is better to experience the pain of a minute or that of a few days!' The person replied, 'Shaykh, I repent, I have understood.'

Special Relationship or Connection (*Nisbat*)

Our Mashā'ikh ﷺ have stated that a special relationship and connection with Allah ﷻ known in the terminology of spirituality as *nisbat* is acquired after much striving. In this elevated stage, the servant is always aware of the presence of Allah ﷻ, always remembering Allah ﷻ, always obedient to Allah ﷻ, this is *nisbat*.

Shaykh Ashraf 'Ali Thānwi ﷺ has explained this with an example. In the Indian Sub-Continent villages, ladies gather to carry numerous water pots from the communal well to their homes. Some will be carrying up to four pots balanced upon their heads, all the time they are talking, joking and gossiping. However, they never drop the containers because their attention is still focused on the task in hand. Likewise a car driver is motoring but at the same time talking, joking, laughing, however not for a moment does his attention turn away.

Similarly, after a period of striving (*mujahadah*) and spiritual exercise (*riyaadhat*) a person acquires this special bond (*nisbat*), however this relationship is broken by certain acts, one of them being lustful gazing. In the realm of spiritual sojourn, the common obstacles and impediments are lustful gazing, haram and doubtful morsels and company of the impious.

Curse Upon The Voyeur & Poser

Lustful gazing is a medium for acquiring the Curse (*la'nat*) of Allah ﷻ. Rasoolullah ﷺ narrated,

> *'Whoever observes with lustful gaze is cursed as well as the person (poser) being observed.'* (*Mishkāt*)

A question which often arises is it is easy to understand why the voyeur is cursed, but why is the poser also being cursed? The 'Ulama have written about the person who is being viewed, 'She too encouraged being ogled at by her demeanour, dress, exposure and body language.' When a man or woman dress to appeal to the opposite non-Mahram gender, obviously they are planning to sin, this is why both the voyeur and poser are being cursed.

The Curse of Allah ﷻ is a very dangerous occurrence; its mere appearance or presence in a vicinity is precarious. Once Rasoolullah ﷺ was travelling in a caravan when an associate cursed an accompanying camel. Instantly, Rasoolullah ﷺ ordered the camel be separated from the caravan as a cursed object should not remain within our midst. (Muslim)

It Is Possible To Fool Humans But...

Allah ﷻ says in the Glorious Qur'ān:

> *'...Undoubtedly, the ears, eyes and heart, of each of them one shall be interrogated.'* (17:36)

Many people labour under the misconception nobody becomes aware of their surreptitious glances just like a child becomes brazen and naughty if he thinks his father will not become aware.

However, Allah ﷻ is aware of the inappropriateness of the gaze; you may be able to fool your companions when you surreptitiously glance at the passing non-mahram; however He is Knower of the Seen and Unseen; how could you deceive Him? This is why the cure for lustful gazing is also mentioned in the Glorious Qur'ān, to reflect upon the observance of Allah ﷻ.

Our pious have stated if you are sitting somewhere and a pretty lady were to pass; however, your father, ustadh or Shaykh are also sitting nearby with their gaze focussed upon you, will you dare to turn your head and vision towards the pretty woman? Never, in the presence of elders; in the presence of your father; your ustadh; your Shaykh, your mind would ruminate over what they will think of you if they notice you ogling at a non-mahram woman?

Similarly, if a junior is sitting near to an elder, would the latter ogle at a non-mahram? If a child, student or mureed are sitting next to their father, ustadh or Shaykh, would the elder stare at a passing lady? The elder would consider, 'What will my son think of me? My father has reached this advanced age and is still ogling at non-mahram women?' 'What will my students think of me?' 'What will my mureed's think of me?'

On account of shame neither would a junior or elder gaze at a non-mahram in each other's presence; whereas in reality by being found-out by any of them, our existence does not grind to a halt; our life and sustenance is not in their control; our Hereafter is not within their grip. At most their opinion of us will be lowered; no more. Why are we so petrified of other's yet brazen with Allah ﷻ who is Forever observing us; has Full Control over our existence and sustenance?

Whereas our belief is stipulated in the Glorious Quran:

'Does he not know Allah is watching (him)?' (96:14)

The Mashā'ikh have formulated a meditation (*muraqabah*) upon this, to constantly ponder that Allah ﷻ is watching us.

CCTV Camera

This is easily understood from an example. Consider you are alone in a Masjid, no other person present, however CCTV cameras are active; operators are viewing us from another location. A non-mahram now happens to pass by, nevertheless although we are alone, one will not have the impudence to view her because we know we are being observed. Similarly, Allah ﷻ outlines in the Glorious Qur'ān the prescription for saving oneself from lustful gazing:

'He knows the treachery of the eyes and whatever is concealed by hearts.' (40:19)

Not only is He ﷻ aware of the movements of our eyes but also our corresponding thoughts and; obviously when He ﷻ is aware of all this, He ﷻ will bring us to account and castigate.

Allah ﷻ is Ever-Watchful

We are able to deceive fellow beings because even their gaze is not perfect, sooner or later their focus will change or weaken, we are then able to view and ogle without them knowing. However, Allah ﷻ is Fully Focused at all times:

'Surely, your Lord is Ever Watchful.' (89:14)

Before a hunter or marksman presses the trigger of his weapon, his thoughts, vision and gaze are fully focused on the target; this focussing is known as *mirsad* (Ever-Watchful), when one becomes oblivious to everything else; total concentration. Allah ﷻ is fully focused on our behaviour and thoughts; if this awareness becomes a reality in our heart, will we be able to ogle or gaze lustfully?

Our Akabireen were living proofs of this awareness, they were ever so cautious that we find it impossible to comprehend. Rasoolullah ﷺ was an example of this behaviour. 'Allamah Yafa'ee ﷺ relates, 'When the

Clan of Abdul-Qais from Bahrain arrived in the Company of Rasoolullah ﷺ, there was a young beardless boy amongst them. He was ordered by Rasoolullah ﷺ to sit behind him ﷺ, despite being sinless he ﷺ was conveying to us a lesson, because Rasoolullah ﷺ also narrated, 'The Ummah of Sayyiduna Dawood ﷻ became embroiled in this fitnah.' (Targheeb)

Caution of Imām Ahmad bin Hambal ﷺ

An *amrad* is such a young boy, upon whose face a few hairs of the moustache are present but no beard; an adolescent boy who may appeal to both men and women and therefore may constitute a fitnah. A person came into the company of Imām Ahmad bin Hambal ﷺ with his young son, an *amrad*. Imām Ahmad ﷺ commented, 'Do not bring him in future.' Other people present queried, 'Shaykh! Why such emphasis?' Imām Ahmad ﷺ commented, 'My elders and *akabir* have emphasised to me to never let a beardless boy in my presence and to save myself from them.'

Caution of Sufyan al-Thawri ﷺ

Sufyan al-Thawri ibn Sa'eed ﷺ (716-778) was a *tābi'i*, leading Muhaddith and *faqeeh* of his time. Once he entered a *hammam* wherein the caretaker sent an *amrad* to pour water and be of service. Instantly, Sufyan al-Thawri ﷺ exclaimed, 'Quickly remove him from here; I witness one Shaytan with a woman and twelve to thirteen Shaytan with this *amrad*.' Hakam bin Zakwan ﷺ used to say, 'There is appeal in the face of an amrad as there is in the face of a young lady, if not a greater attraction, therefore save yourself from their company.'

Imam Muslee ﷺ used to say, 'I have heard forty saints, who were known as Qutb and Abdal, laying great emphasis on this, accordingly there should be a strenuous effort to save oneself from lustful gazing.'

Shaykh Ashraf 'Ali Thānwi ☼ used to narrate, 'When travelling by train and two carriages happen to pass or stop at crossings or platforms at railway stations, then if I am sitting next to the window, I will not look into the adjacent train carriage because it is possible females travelling in the other train are sitting with faces exposed assuming nobody will be able to observe us.'

Eyes Become Polluted by Adulterous Glances

Shaykh-ul-Hadeeth Zakariyya ☼ used to state, 'When a person sins, then certain pious servants of Allah ☼ are made aware of such misdemeanour, however Allah ☼ has also bestowed the latter with magnanimity and His Attribute of concealment (*sattari*) whereby they never publicise these faults.'

A person entered the gathering of Sayyidduna 'Uthman ☼ having taken a lustful glance at a non-mahram along the way. 'Uthman ☼ immediately saw signs from his eyes and face, however he reproached the entire gathering not the individual, 'What has become of people! They enter the *Majlis* in such a condition that adultery drips from their eyes.'

Shaykh Mufti Mahmood Gangohi ☼ used to relate, 'Once Shaykh 'Abdur-Raheem Raipoori ☼ was making ablution when two visitors arrived; one a mureed, the other his accomplice.

Observing his mureed, Shaykh 'Abdur-Raheem Raipoori ☼ commented, 'You have not lost anything despite the laziness which appears to accompany humans.' Turning to his companion, 'There is one impediment in your heart, the other in your eyes.' It transpired the mureed was inconsistent in his devotional practises, whilst his companion was submerged in lustful gazing as well as harbouring corrupted aqeedah (belief).

Ladies Are Veiled Treasures

Shaykh Ashraf 'Ali Thānwi ☙ used to narrate, 'Some people are so protective of their daughters that even their neighbours are unaware whether there is a young lady living next door. They and the neighbourhood would only find out when the time of nikah arrived, 'Really, they had a daughter as well?' This is how much attention and priority was given to upbringing girls in purdah.

Whereas nowadays according to Shaykh Qāri Siddique Bandhwi ☙ the sad state of our *Muāsharah* is such that, 'Young Muslim ladies leave for work early in the morning not returning till late evening; with families not knowing how their daughter's day has transpired. However, if the family pet goes missing for even a short while, the entire family (parents, siblings, grandparents, uncles and aunts) all go around the neighbourhood searching and wailing.'

Modesty, Honour & Nobility

It appears in Hadeeth that Rasoolullah ﷺ possessed such modesty, honour and nobility akin to a young maiden diffidently sitting within the confines of her home. Yesteryear such was the prudence and care adopted with our young ladies; in complete contrast, today girls come and go as they please in full view of their parents; without the latter raising even an eyelid.

Where Has Our Honour Disappeared?

'Allamah ibn-ul-Hajj Maliki ☙ has written about the state of Egyptian ladies some five centuries ago, however it would appear to be a foreboding of our times, 'They travel to shops with outsiders, freely converse with shopkeepers and walk flirtingly displaying their wares, all with the silent approval of their husband, father and mother; who display no remorse or guilt.'

Opportunity of Adultery For Every Person

It appears in Hadeeth that Allah ﷻ has written a portion of adultery for every person to be involved therein: adultery of the eyes is to view a non-mahram. Shaykh Salman Mansurpoori *hafizahullah* has explained this very elaborately, 'In every person's life occasions arise wherein he may become embroiled in adultery; his eyes may become involved; his ears may become involved; his tongue may become involved.' For some pious servants one does wonder how they could ever become involved, however such occasions do occur in every person's life. For example, in today's culture, who is able to protect his vision? Look all around us; on billboards, on buildings, on streets, on public transport, within the house, on newspapers, on leaflets, on mail, on cereal and soap boxes, on bottles and every kind of merchandising and packaging to the extent if you purchase a small bottle of medicine, toothpaste or shampoo, even here there will be the picture or outline of a woman. How may a person save himself? There are those, who being blessed with tawfeeq from Allah ﷻ do save themselves, as for those who commit shortcomings therein, they should repent and try their utmost to amend.

Noble Examples

Shaykh-ul-Hadeeth Zakariyya ﷺ narrates, 'Shaykh Qamruddeen ﷺ who was the Imam of Jāme Masjid, Saharanpur once became ill. In his place Shaykh Muhammad Ilyas ﷺ (the founder of *Tableegh Jama'at* and a senior lecturer at Mazahir Uloom, Saharanpur) would deputise.

He would leave before Asr Salah and return after leading Maghrib. Sometimes I used to accompany him and noted how from the moment he left the Darul Uloom until he arrived at the Masjid his gaze would be focussed upon his feet. Similarly, Shaykh Khaleel Ahmad Saharanpuri ﷺ would also always keep his gaze focussed on the ground.'

First Chance Glance is Forgiven Nevertheless It Is Harmful

Rasoolullah ﷺ advised Sayyidduna 'Ali ؓ,

> *'O Ali! Do not glance a second time after the first. The first is forgiven however the second in sinful.'* (Mishkaat)

Although the first chance gaze is forgiven, nevertheless it too is not without harm. Moreover, although these pious Shuyookh mentioned above were also aware of this Hadeeth, they were so cautious as to avoid even the first chance glance. Why? Because it is possible the first chance glance arouses a desire and allows a thought to settle in the heart. If you eat poison by accident or unknowingly, obviously there is no sin, even so the poison will surely take effect.

Ask any Mufti if somebody had eaten poison by mistake and dies, is he sinful, will his death be described as suicide? The answer will obviously be no, however what benefit is such an answer and outcome to the dead person? The poison took its toll.

Similarly, although the first chance glance is forgiven, it is likely to create an effect, this is why it is important to keep one's gaze lowered as far as possible.

Employment Issues/Shaykh Mufti Ahmad Khanpoori's Reply

Question: I am employed in a government office wherein I have to work and talk with ladies. As they are non-mahram am I sinning?

Answer: A person should make a firm resolution to save himself from sin. Shaykh Mufti Muhammad Taqee *hafizahullah* relates about his patron Shaykh Dr. 'Abdul-Hai 'Arifee ؓ, who was a lawyer, however because he was not happy with his income from law, he decided to become a homeopathic doctor. However, here women patients would visit for diagnoses and treatment, which presented another dilemma. Shaykh Dr. 'Abdul-Hai 'Arifee ؓ relates, 'I therefore conditioned myself to keep my gaze lowered at all times not lifting them for one moment. I was so cautious that I would not even know who the patient was; whoever came and described their predicament, I would diagnose and thereafter prescribe a course of treatment. After a while no difficulty was noticeable.'

If a person is diagnosed as suffering from TB and doctors prohibit him from smoking, then he will have to forgo cigarettes. This lustful gazing is just as dangerous for our Imaan as TB is for the body, we will have to save ourselves and undertake abstention, and suffer the indignation of a bitter remedy.

Pleasure in Striving

Those who chew tobacco in betel leaf derive great pleasure there from. However, those unacquainted with this practise are unable to tolerate even a small amount of tobacco in the mouth, they find it nauseating and revolting. In complete contrast, the habitual eater cannot make do without tobacco and betel leaf.

Similar is the state of our *nafs*, it derives pleasure from what it is accustomed to; if it is habitual in lustful gazing, it derives pleasure there from, however, the resultant turmoil of the heart, agitation and palpation within the body are excruciating.

In complete contrast, the person who undertakes the trouble to keep his gaze lowered although experiences an initial difficulty, nevertheless derives long term happiness and pleasure in this striving.

Sayyidduna Abu Darda ؓ used to comment, 'I desire to live in this world, not to acquire wealth, but to ascertain the pleasure of fasting during long hot days.' An apparently difficult task is providing pleasure, however for this to take place some bitterness of a few days will need to be tolerated.

Our *nafs* is allegorical to a toddler accustomed to only milk. When the time arrives for the toddler to be weaned away; the mother has to experience days of turmoil. The toddler will throw tantrums and not sleep at night, nor allow his mother or the rest of the household to sleep either. Everybody will become vexed, however if the mother takes false pity and gives-in to his tantrums then he will never be weaned away from milk. Why is the toddler crying? He considers he is being deprived from his favourite item, milk, little realising what he is about to receive in exchange, various types of foodstuff, is infinitely greater, more tastier, delicious and satisfying. He has until today only tasted milk.

Similarly, our *nafs* has been submerged in lustful gazing, when it forgoes this infancy, Allah 🕌 will bestow such spiritual pleasures and ecstasy which are indescribable and incomprehensible.

Likewise, the person misfortunate to suffer from rash, finds scratching the itch a temporary relief and relieving; little realising every scratch intensifies and worsens the rash. Medicine will need to be applied and for the remedy to work courage, patience, self-discipline and a complete ban on scratching will need to be imposed. Within a few days complete relief and recovery will Insha'Allah be experienced; such healing, good health and comfort will be enjoyed in whose presence the relief of scratching will pail into naught.

Allah 🕌 has created tranquillity in His 🕌 obedience and worship; this is His 🕌 Favour for the peace, composure and serenity this brings is not possible in any worldly pursuit or means. Therefore although controlling one's gaze is initially difficult, nevertheless the rewards and contentment bestowed on undertaking such toil are much greater.

May Allah 🕌 grant all of us tawfeeq.

Chapter Three

Protect Your Eyes

by

$\mathcal{S}$haykh Mufti Muhammad Taqee 'Uthmani

hafizahullah

Reviewed by

Mawlana Qāri Yousuf Patel

'We did offer the Trust to the Heavens and earth and the mountains, but they refused to bear its burden and were afraid of it but man picked it up. Indeed he is unjust (to himself), unaware (of the end).'   (Glorious Qur'ān, 33:72)

'Today the Muslim home has become a drive-in cinema and theatre. From dawn until dusk the doors are locked as everybody travels away for work, study and leisure. Come the evening people return according to their schedule to view and eat in front of widescreens before retiring to sleep.'

$\mathcal{A}$llah ﷻ relates in the Glorious Qur'ān:

> *'Successful indeed are the Believers. Who concentrate with attention and humbleness when offering salāh (prayer). And who keep themselves away from futility. And who are performers of zakat. And those who guard their chastity (private parts). Except from their wives or (slaves) that their right hand possess, for then they are free from blame. However, those who seek (sexual pleasure) beyond that are the transgressors.'* (23:1-7)

The Glorious Qur'ān describes as successful those Believers who safeguard their chastity except from their spouse. Any other form of sexual gratification is beyond limits and a form of oppression on one's own soul. Islam is a complete mode of living wherein even natural sexual inclinations have been catered for in the *halāl*, pure, wholesome form of nikah, which brings reward and tremendous blessings. Any sexual activity outside of nikah is haram and a means of turmoil and ultimately self-destruction.

Maghreb Culture

Those cultures which have moved away from marital sexual relationships have suffered socially, spiritually, physically and morally. Today, the world is having the Maghreb culture thrust upon it; however because they have abandoned nikah and sought to seek sexual gratification beyond the norms of marriage, their sexual exploits are those of base animals. In some of these Maghreb countries, between sixty and seventy percent of births are recorded as illegitimate; a necessary corollary of this is either weakening or breakdown in the centuries old family structure: relationships between parents, children and siblings are either strained or have collapsed. The think-tanks and intelligentsia of these cultures are screaming for a solution as they witness themselves on the brink of social and moral destruction. This is because they have abandoned the Divine Qur'ānic way of fulfilling sexual inclinations through nikah.

No End To Sexual Deviation

Allah ﷻ has created such a system whereby if these sexual inclinations are channelled through nikah in the right way then they are a means for human progression and comfort. However, the moment these inclinations transgress lawful and permissible limits, then this very sexual disorientation unleashes an insatiable and unquenchable appetite. Whenever a person indulges in any form of haram sexual demeanour, then a necessary result is abandonment of norms and lack of true gratification. With each successive act of misbehaviour his appetite remains unappeased; just like the person suffering from oedema (illness of water retention in the body); no amount of water quenches such a person's thirst and only increases the swelling, discomfort, pain and water build up in the body.

Lack of Tranquillity

In Maghreb cultures, despite removing all natural boundaries of sexual behaviour and indulging in hedonism, tranquillity is not achieved. With every successive act of sexual deviation, the ultimate goal of succour appears afar. Events and episodes have reached such a state where numerous are the incidents of individuals not only raping a woman but not finding gratification until they have murdered her in a gruesome manner. This is the unique state of Maghreb culture; they have forced open the door to outside world for women; devalued her personality and transformed her into an object of appeal to all and sundry. In those countries where women are 'fully liberated,' the incidents of rape are not only infinitely higher but so are the figures for murder where sex was the primary motive. It is not enough to fulfil the desires by promiscuity and adultery; a further urge and craving is there to forcefully rape women; thereafter even this is not enough, an additional bestial and sadistic compulsion leads to the gruesome abuse (and sometimes even murder) of the raped victim.

The Glorious Qur'ān advocates nikah and warns of the dangers and perils of acting beyond the limits of the pure institution of marriage. Sexual relationship within nikah is not only lauded but is a means of acquiring reward (*thawab*).

First Limit - Protecting & Guarding Gaze

To save one from impermissible avenues, Allah ﷻ has appointed limits and boundaries. If these are adhered to then a person will never become involved in sexual depravity. The first limit is protecting and safeguarding one's gaze. Rasoolullah ﷺ commented,

> *'The lustful gaze is an arrow from the arrows of Shaytan. Whosoever, on account of My Fear forgoes it, I shall transform it into such sweetness which he will experience in his heart.'* (Tabrānee)

A necessary corollary of lustful gazing is incorrect and wicked desires and thoughts within the heart; such orientation which lead a person astray.

Qur'ānic Prescription

> *'Tell the believing men that they must lower their gazes and guard their private parts...'* (Glorious Quran, 24:30)

This is the first Qur'ānic prescription for protecting one's chastity; to deliberately glance at a non-mahram is the first step of adultery. In a Hadeeth Rasoolullah ﷺ stated,

'The eyes too commit adultery and their adultery is to ogle at (non-mahram).'

Bounty of Vision

This eyesight which Allah ﷻ has bestowed to you, reflect upon its structure, mechanism and functioning. From birth until death it operates without any servicing or effort and for free; it allows you to view any item you choose. Only when Allah ﷻ grants somebody an opportunity to reflect and study the wonderful functions of this organ, does a person begin to appreciate the complexities therein. Even those highly skilled Eye Consultants who have dedicated their entire lives to the study and treatment of eye orders are still at a loss to fully explain its composition or *modus operandi*.

The day, Allah ﷻ forbid, some problem with our vision is experienced, a tremor runs throughout our body and existence; what if we were to loose our eyesight? A person who has vision issues is prepared to spend the entire wealth of this world to have it restored whereby he is able to view his wife, children, parents, siblings, relatives, friends and associates.

Even a weakening of eyesight, double-vision, flickering, squinting, cross or lazy eye is enough to send us rushing to an eye specialist in an attempt to have this defect corrected. However, this priceless bounty which is granted to us from birth unto death is an unbelievably complex organ working automatically without any input from us.

Moreover it is probably the most sensitive organ in our body. One notices, whenever a piece of grit or speck of dust enters the eye, what discomfort, panic, anxiety and pain this cause.

The eyes have been perfectly located in the human body; protected on all sides by a defence system *par excellence*. A complex bone structure surrounds it on all sides, thereafter eye brows and finally eye lashes. All this encapsulated in a face of immense beauty. Such an outstanding formwork from Allah ﷻ without any effort on our part; all we are asked to do is use it in an appropriate manner; you are merely forbidden to employ it in those arenas wherein is your own spiritual destruction. View the earth, heavens, skies, oceans, mountains, rivers, orchards, flowers and any other good. View your wife, parents, children, siblings, families and friends, however save yourself from viewing only two: a non-mahram and anybody else with contempt. These are the only two restrictions being applied, you are free to view everything else.

Conditions Upon Restoration of Vision

In modern society it is admittedly difficult to find refuge for the eyes; for trials and tribulations surround us all side. The modern Muslim complains it is extremely difficult to control one's gaze from such factors. However, if a person, Allah ﷻ forbid were to loose his vision and one of the conditions for having it restored was the prohibition of viewing a small number of objects; then undoubtedly any sane person would happily agree to this pre-condition.

We are merely being ordered to not view certain matters; all other items we are not only allowed to view but we gain reward for viewing many of them. For example, when a person views his parents with the gaze of affection and respect, Allah ﷻ grants this person the reward of one Hajj and one Umrah. Similarly, when a person views his or her spouse with affection , then Allah ﷻ looks upon both of them with His Mercy. Notice how employing the gaze correctly earns tremendous reward and spiritual elevation. Using it incorrectly is described as amongst the arrows of Shaytan and a means of spiritual destruction and punishment.

Act With Courage

In the final analysis when a person employs his gaze in ogling at forbidden objects then it is pure blindness; he has already forfeited true vision:

> *'But whoever is (too) blind in this (world to see the right path) will be (too) blind in the Hereafter (to reach salvation), and much more astray from the path.'*

(Glorious Qur'an, 17:72)

Accordingly whenever a person makes a firm resolution to not employ his vision incorrectly, then Allah ﷻ, who has created tremendous strength in a person's will power, grants blessings and progress. As long as Muslims acted in accordance with the Qur'ānic prescription offered by Allah ﷻ they continued to enjoy success and were protected from turmoil and disgrace. My late respected father, Shaykh Mufti Muhammad Shafee' ﷺ has related a historical incident during the rule of Sayyidduna 'Umar Farooq ؓ. Sayyidduna Abu 'Ubaidah ibn al-Jarrāh ؓ (583-638 CE), was amongst the ten *'Asharah Mubasharah* and the Ameer of *Shām* (Syria, Palestine & Jordan). The Muslims, under his leadership, had surrounded a Byzantine fort and stronghold in *Shām*; however the siege dragged on for some considerable time. When the Byzantines realised the Muslims were not for moving they concocted a strategy. They sent a message to Sayyidduna Abu 'Ubaidah ibn al-Jarrāh ؓ notifying him of their decision to surrender and allow the Muslim Army to enter through the city gates, march through the mall containing shops and up to the Royal Palace.

In the meantime, they drew up a strategy. Being aware of the long time the Muslim army had been away from Arabia and their families, they encouraged all the young maidens of the locality to dress up and stand provocatively outside along the mall with a view to enticing the soldiers and distracting them towards rape, pillage, plunder and loot as usually happens when an enemy town is overrun. This would give the Byzantine army an opportunity to attack from the rear and defeat the Muslims.

Beware The Spiritual Insight of Mu'min

When Muslims practice upon Deen then Allah ﷻ grants spiritual vision and insight (*firasat*). Rasoolullah ﷺ commented,

> *'Be alert to the insight of the Mu'min, he views with the núr of Allah.'*

When the Byzantine terms of surrender were read out to Sayyidduna Abu 'Ubaidah ibn al-Jarrāh ؓ he became suspicious, 'Until now they stiffly resisted, all of a sudden they wish to surrender even opening the main gates and allowing us to march unopposed along the mall to the palace?' Nevertheless, he accepted the surrender and then summoned his entire army of a few thousand soldiers and delivered a sermon:

> *'It is only through the Favours and Grace of Allah ﷻ that the enemy have surrendered and are inviting us to enter the city. You should undoubtedly enter, however I wish to recite a Verse of the Glorious Qur'ān unto you which you should act upon as you enter,*
>
> **'Tell the believing men that they must lower their gazes and guard their private parts...'** *(Glorious Qur'ān, 24:30)*

Accordingly, the entire army entered the city reciting this Verse, looking down at their feet. Not one soul raised his gaze to look hither-thither at the trappings on either side.

Amazed, all the city dwellers exclaimed with one voice, 'What creation is this? Any army which enters a city as victors commences a rout of anarchy?' Many of the onlookers accepted Islam witnessing this spectacle. This is how Islam spread and was propagated by the Sahābah.

Four Avenues of Attack

Shaykh Ashraf 'Ali Thānwi ﷺ used to narrated, 'When Allah ﷻ ousted Shaytan from Paradise (Jannah) and condemned him, he ignominiously boasted, 'When You have thrown me out of Paradise and accepted my du'a of a life until the Day of Qiyāmah, then I will lay await to deviate the children of Adam ﷺ who was the cause of my rejection in this way;'

> *'He said, 'Now you have led me astray, 'I will certainly sit for them (in ambush) on Your straight path. Then I will come upon them from their front side and from their rear, and from their right and from their left. You will not find most of them grateful.'* (Glorious Qur'ān, 7:16-17)

Shaykh Ashraf 'Ali Thānwi ﷺ continues, 'Shaytan forgot to mention two directions; from above and below. Accordingly, he ambushes from four sides; however protection is either from above or below. Establish a relationship with Allah ﷻ above; incline (ruju) towards Him and seek His Assistance. Thereafter keep your gaze lowered, Allah ﷻ will keep you protected.'

A lustful gaze wreaks havoc spiritually; moreover it is so rampant in our society that perchance there maybe one or two who are saved from this malady. All around us we are surrounded by the call to view, to ogle, to stare, to gawk, to glance, to gaze. The culture established by Rasoolullah ﷺ was one of modesty, purity, chastity, diffidence, shame, honour and dignity containing a high moral code of behaviour and conduct. This is in complete contrast to today's hedonistic, brash, gaudy, chauvinistic, bigoted and arrogant pomposity which surrounds us.

Another fatal development is our weaker resolution and lack of self-discipline, self-motivation and the self-awareness within Muslim's to take stock of their behaviour, conduct and the realisation that we are to stand before our Creator and answer for our deeds.

Poem

Shaykh Mufti Muhammad Taqee 'Uthmāni

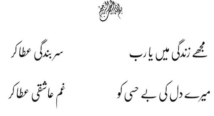

سر بندگی عطا کر   مجھے زندگی میں یارب

غم عاشقی عطا کر   میرے دل کی بے حسی کو

In this life O Creator grant me privilege & honour of the servitude of Yours;
grant my restless heart the pangs of affection of Yours.

تیری یاد کی کسک ہو   تیرے درد کی چبک ہو

میرے دل کی دھڑکنوں کو   نئی یہ کلی عطا کر

Brilliance of Your remembrance be, affliction of Your commemoration be;
grant the dread of my heart a new restlessness to see.

جو مجھے تیرا پتہ دے   جو تجھ ہی سے لو لگا دے

مجھے گم رہی عطا کر   میرے عہد کی زباں میں

Enjoins my devotion to You whoever, highlights my shortcomings whoever;
my promise and word be granted consideration forever.

وہی روشنی عطا کر   جو دلوں میں نور کر دے

Whatever lightens my heart, grant me this brilliance apart;

میں یہی یہ کھو نہ جاؤں   میں سفر میں سو نہ جاؤں

کی ہما ہیں عطا کر   مجھے ذوق و شوق منزل

I should not slumber on this sojourn, nor should I falter or get lost in turn;
grant me self-motivation, enthusiasm and craving unto destination return

رگِ جان کی مسافت   بڑی دور ہے ابھی تک

جو دیا ہے قربِ تو نے   تو شعور بھی عطا کر

Remains afar yet the jugular veins expanse;
What proximity You have endowed; grant appreciation perchance;

نہ ہوا آشنا کسی سے   بھری انجمن میں رہ کر

مجھے دوست کے بھرم ٹ   میں وہ بے کسی عطا کر

Even when in lively gatherings, I should not become enjoined to trappings;
whilst in the company of friends; grant me aloofness from trends;

میرے دل میں تو ہی تو ہو   مجھے تیری جستجو ہو

میرے قلب کو وہ فیض   درِ عارفی عطا کر

You should be my quest; in my heart be You and only Your pursuit;
grant my heart the blessings and pangs of knowledge of Yours to suit.

مجھے زندگی میں یا رب   سرِ بندگی عطا کر

میرے دل کی بے حسی کو   غمِ عاشقی عطا کر

In this life O Creator grant me privilege & honour of the servitude of Yours;
Grant my restless heart the pangs of affection of Yours.

Kindly transcribed in Urdu by Mufti Shabbaz Ahmad of Edinburgh damat barakatuhum
& Translated in English by Amanah Studio

haykh Maseehullah Khan ۝ narrated,

'There was a laundryman whose family business catered for the washing and ironing needs of their locality. They also received clothes from the Royal Household for cleaning and pressing. Observing the resplendent clothes of the charming unmarried Princess, the laundryman's young son, despite not having viewed her beauty, became infatuated with her: 'If her clothes are like this what must she be like!' Day by day, his condition deteriorated until he was reduced to a pale figure of his former self. He stopped eating, drinking and sleeping. Thoughts of this Princess haunted him all the time. Observing his pitiful condition, out of naivety, one day his mother exclaimed, 'Don't you know the Princess has passed away, so stop thinking about her and get on with your life.'

Immediately, upon hearing this news he fell into a swoon, collapsed and died.

Clothes from the Royal Household continued to arrive at the laundry, they were washed and returned. However, the Princess noticed they were not being pressed with as much attention as before and came to quiz the laundrywoman, 'Mother! My clothes do not come back like before, pray tell me why?' 'O it's nothing dear.' 'No, you must tell me.' The laundrywoman replied, 'Dear, my son became obsessed upon observing your clothes; he used to spend hours washing and pressing them, not eating, drinking or sleeping. One day, in order to remove him from his predicament, I blurted out that you had passed away. Straight away he fell unconscious and died. This is why your dresses do not arrive with the same dedication and service as before.' Immediately, upon hearing this, the Princess fell ill and within three days she too passed away.

Despite neither having viewed the other; merely observing an indication of beauty or some other personal feature is enough to effect a person's spiritual, mental and physical equilibrium. This is why Imam Aboo Haneefah ۝ advised, 'When a ghair-mahram lady arises from her place of sitting, do not sit in the same place until the warmth from her sitting has disappeared.'

Chapter Four

Misuse of Internet, Social Networking Forums & Online Video Games

'Silver glistens white and new, but blackens the hands, clothes and you.' (Shah Jalalluddeen Rumi ﷺ)

'The Information Age offers much to mankind, and I would like to think that we will rise to the challenges it presents. But it is vital to remember that information - in the sense of raw data - is not knowledge, that knowledge is not wisdom, and that wisdom is not foresight...' (Arthur C. Clarke)

'...The internet is a way of being sexually addicted but it does not cause the addiction. What causes it is the relationship between the child and their parents. Almost always they are maternally (not materially) deprived.' (Thaddeus Birchard)

Salat and Salams upon the Final Messenger ﷺ

Allah ﷻ mentions in the Glorious Qur'an:

> *'O Believers! Fear Allah and join the company of the truthful.'*

Nabee ﷺ commented,

> *'...like a (train of) hundred camels. Only one of them capable of mounting and riding.' (Tirmidhi)*

> *'In proximity to Qiyamah (Day of Judgement), cataclysms will appear as if beads falling from a rosary (tasbeeh).'*

Shaykh Dr. Abdul-Hayy 'Arifee ﷺ narrated, 'Everyday we witness a new upheaval. We have enough worldly tribulations but are now witnessing such deeni commotion from people who adopt a deeni hue and platform; who themselves are astray and lead others astray. They are only interested in modernity; how to confirm their brand of Islam to suit alien models; Muslims should remain Muslim in name only to pacify others. This alien ideology is one of total fulfilment of every desire, glamour, abundance, extravagance, comfort, affluence, self-indulgence, mirth and merriment. No thought is given to whether any matter is permissible or impermissible; whether Allah ﷻ or His Rasool ﷺ have given us permission to participate. Whatever the fad of the hour, we have to blindly follow, otherwise we will be counted amongst the backward. When modesty and chastity depart there is not much hope for *Imaan* because immorality, immodesty, bashfulness and hedonism are then no longer considered sins; they are accepted as normal, in keeping with the times and norms of society.'

There is now a generation of Muslim Youth (estimated 1 million in the UK alone) who have not experienced a life without the Internet and mobile phone. As online mediums have become widely available, ubiquitous and classified as a 'human right' (by the United Nations) one of the greatest dangers to Muslim Youth is unlimited, easy accessibility and vulnerability to inappropriate online games, websites and social networking forums. What begins as 'innocent' playing of games, chatting with friends online, viewing of cartoons, documentaries, sports, news and even Islamic naats and lectures sooner or later leads unto the viewing of unsavoury images (irrespective of whether this is described as viral, soft or hard) and association with impious people.

Difference Between TV & Online Mediums

Online mediums have a greater 'pull' than TV and appears to effect people much quicker. Consequently, family interaction, the ability to practice good deeds (*amal saleh*), association with the pious and acquisition of Deeni Knowledge declines dramatically and, this drop is directly proportional to the increase in Internet use and playing of video games. Why? Like a city centre, the Web has neighbourhoods and avenues; some undoubtedly useful and informative, many others useless, evil and lethal. Even a casual or accidental venture down one of the slippery strands for a few seconds or minutes exposes the viewer to such wicked depravity; which is, at times more corrosive than the seedier parts of Amsterdam, Rio de Janeiro, Bangkok, Tokyo or Shanghai.

Indisputably there are many benefits in Internet usage and votaries will claim even in video games (it keeps children and adults pacified; though intoxicated would be a better description) nevertheless Muslim Children are experiencing many harmful effects to their outlook and Deeni orientation as well as suffering physical and behavioural effects. One medical doctor and educator believes this obsession with video games, violence, aggression and pornography actually affects the brains of young people,

> 'Gary Rose, M.D., President of the M.I.S.H., located in Austin, Texas, has recently revealed research concerning the development of the brain. "...We now know, through MRI studies-magnetic resonance imaging studies that are not harmful to do-that the pre-frontal cortex, the front part of the brain, is the last part of the brain to mature. That is the part of the brain that deals with long term judgment and delayed gratification... By scanning multiple brains, we have shown it is not really mature until about age 25.'

Video Games & Social Networking

Social networking forums, websites, video and online games are extremely profitable for service providers but at what physical, neurological, social, economic, moral and spiritual costs to our children?

We now have a generation of disorientated, disaffected, troubled, disengaged and dissatisfied Muslim young; who appear to have no Deeni inclination or true ambition to excel in life in any field and whom we are about to lose. The live for now, credit card generation appears in slumber, mesmerised into a constant state of adolescence; disrespecting parents' yet dependent upon their support and finances; drifting aimlessly from one fad, gizmo, video game, designer ware to another; lacking in motivation, self-discipline, restraint, self-esteem and self-belief, constantly underperforming and idle. Their GCSE, A-level and Degree results are no reflection of their aptitude, competence, common sense, intelligence, entrepreneurship, ability to earn a living, support a family or contribute to humanity. What use will such a generation of idle Muslim youth be to society or to prospective spouses looking for partners and parent for their children? Too many Muslim households are shaking their heads in dismay and disbelief; too many Muslim parents at a loss to explain their children's behaviour.

Affluence and a perceived automatic entitlement to rights (*huqqoq*) without any sense of reciprocating obligations seems to be the order of the day in a community which is living upon the fruits of sacrifices, graft, savings and investments made by the first and second generation of immigrants and pious half a century ago and the State Welfare System. Muslim's are spending between 30 to 150 hours a week upon Internet and online video games; this is more than the traditional working week which their grandparents spent in mills and factories for a pittance.

How may any community whose youth spend so much time a week on fantasies ever hope to prosper in any avenue of human endeavour? Nations and communities who have become *Imam's* (leaders) in knowledge, science, technology and commerce have always done so through hard work, graft and study. Relates 'Allamah Iqbal ﷺ:

> *'Mature thinking of the nation's preacher has gone.*
>
> *The Muslim's natural panache has gone, fiery speeches have gone.*
>
> *The ritual of Adhan has remained whilst spirit of Bilal ؓ has gone.*
>
> *Philosophy has persisted, the teaching of Ghazzali ﷺ has gone.'*

Aggression & Desensitisation

Video games have reached a point where participants become immersed in virtual fantasies and this 'alternative world' haunts avid players henceforth. The supposedly family-friendly nature of recent online games (Wii, Xbox 360 and PS3) has brought gaming out of the bedroom and into the living rooms of the country. In the process it has further exposed Muslim youth to the company of impious because video games have changed dramatically and are inimical towards Islam, its teachings and the pious. When a Muslim spends hours daily shooting people dressed in Sunnah attire, how may such a person be expected to respect his Asatizah, Imam, Ulama, Masha'ikh and Propagators who don the clothing worn by Prophet Muhammad ﷺ, his Companions ؓ and successive generations of Pious (Sulaha ؒ)?

The seeds of rebellion and treachery are being planted and parents are naively buying such game stations and videos which are a threat to their children's Imaan and well-being. Studies show a correlation between video games (estimated 90% of which contain violence) and psychological behaviour. We are witnessing a 'flight' or 'fight' phenomena (both at home, in Makatib and schools), increase in aggressive behaviour, lack of chivalry, assistance and gentlemanly conduct. Players are encouraged to act selfishly in acquiring fictitious credits, to win at all costs even through deception and cheating:

'Cry 'Havoc!' And let slip the dogs of war.'

Over a relatively short period of time players become desensitised to corrupt values; violence, aggression, foul language, uncouth behaviour, drugs, sexual misdemeanour, fraud and music. Why? Almost all video games, unsavoury websites and chat rooms are either written or managed by people of dubious character whose thoughts patterns, outlook, morals and language are sub-consciously accepted and transformed onto the minds of observers, readers and players. In the final analysis, all such avenues are a waste of time because there is neither any worldly or Deeni benefit in them; life is time and time is life.

The danger is not only of 'closet addiction' to video games, social networking and pornography (the viewing of any images or media which arouse desires in an haram manner) but an even greater danger of considering all this as harmless fun; innocent, somehow connected to education, 'part of the internet' mentality, victimless and therefore morally acceptable or inevitable. Due to such exposure, young people are disregarding decades, if not eons of religious and moral beliefs in sexual restriction within a short time. What was considered sacrosanct;

values which were passed down families over generations; from bosom to bosom; the sense of right and wrong, the ethos of Islam, the treasure of all Muslim households, the integrity, the natural (*tabee'*) purity is now being bartered away down cable and wireless connections within a short time for ever. Any voice to the contrary is labelled as prudish (*dakyanus*)

> '*It is now estimated that 12 per cent of our five-to seven-year-olds and 16 per cent of eight-to 17-year-olds have unintentionally stumbled on to some of the estimated 250 million pages of pornography on the internet, while 38 per cent of older teens admit to seeking out such sites.*'

Family Ties & Social Interaction

Studies reveal a fair percentage of chat users form personal relationships with other users; some of these associations result in a face-to-face meeting which thereafter descends into supposedly romantic but in reality adulterous unions. However, because the very basis of such encounters were clandestine, haram and uncultured, the majority of these relationships end up in failure and misery.

Children love video games, why? It appeals to the self (*nafs*) and minds of shallow understanding, is played by peers and encouraged by advertising and the secular education system as being at the forefront of science and technology. The *nafs* relishes any alternative to *Thikrullah* and such digital mediums provide a fantasy outlet; similar to a child's infatuation with toys, however this malady appears to captivate many well into middle-age and beyond. Such games are also now connected to social networking forums; the blight of Facebook, My Space and Twitter; thus allowing people to interconnect with other's far away whilst ignoring those in the same household and room. Such digital outlets contribute towards the modern phenomena of deterioration and breakdown in family relationships and ties. People become so immersed and addicted online they neglect family responsibilities, becoming disrespectful and inimical towards parents and siblings. Salāh with Jamaat, Maktab attendance and revision of lessons, preparation of coursework and examination, household chores and domestic duties all suffer. Moreover the ability to associate with other members of society in the Sunnah manner is affected; notwithstanding the argument presented by participants of interacting with friends online. Communities and families are duped into relinquishing their identities in the name of education and technological progress with the promise of material prosperity and recognition...

> *'Everyone is intoxicated with the wine of indulgence and merry.*
>
> *You have neither the wealth of Uthman ☙ nor the valour of Ali ☙,*
>
> *What spiritual relation then between you and your ancestors to see?'*

Humanity is being channelled along principals of mass-control and conditioned along Pavlovian lines; with each fad and gizmo triggering predictable behaviour patterns. Sayyidduna Sa'eed ibn Khudri ☙ narrates that Prophet Muhammad ﷺ stated,

> **'You will tread the same path as was trodden by those before you, inch by inch and step by step so much so that if they had entered into the hole of the lizard, you would follow them in this also. We said: 'O Prophet of Allah, (do you mean) the (non-muslims)?' He ﷺ replied: 'Who else?'** *(Muslim Shareef)*

Health Issues

Since the mid 80's obesity has become an unparalleled problem in the 'developed' world. Online mediums have contributed to this issue because they encourage a sedentary lifestyle, consumption of junk fast-food and snacks, lack of exercise and consequently increase in obesity. Another frequent occurrence is *Repetitive Strain Injury* (RSI). Even people who spend long hours 'genuinely' working on computers suffer from pain in certain joints; especially wrists, arms, shoulders, back and neck. Video games compound these pains by encouraging the wearing of headsets, loud noises, sudden movements and focussing of eyes to maintain concentration for long periods. Studies have shown a deterioration in children's blink reflex. There have also been reports of increase in epileptic fits and fatal blood clots. Moreover, playing such violent games for a few hours daily disrupts a child's sleep pattern and grossly affects his ability to memorise the Glorious Qur'an, consequently Deeni Lessons and outlook are the first to suffer.

haykh Khaleel Ahmad Saharanpoori 🌼 used to narrate, 'To lustfully gaze at either non-mahram ladies or boys weakens the memory (*quwwat hafizah*). To substantiate this claim the proof of huffaz not being able to remember a seventh portion of the Glorious Qur'an (*Manzil*) or for those students engaged in memorisation their failure to remember lessons is sufficient. When Imām Shafee' 🌼 complained of weakness in his memory to his Ustadh...the latter's reply was beautifully encapsulated in a couplet...

> 'When I complained of weakness in memory to Imam Waqee 🌼, he advised, 'O Student! Save yourself from sins for 'ilm is a celestial light (nur) from Allah 🕮 and this nur from Allah 🕮 is not granted to a sinful person.'

Concentration Span

haykh Maseehullah Khan 🌼 used to narrate, 'Images viewed in childhood years act as blueprint for behaviour later on in life; the day the child's feet are able to act independently, they will steer him in whatever direction they were programmed to in infanthood.' When young infants and children are allowed unlimited access to video games and online mediums, the flashing bright lights, buzzing humming noises and sounds affect the development of their brains;

especially their concentration spans and faculty of memorisation. Youngsters constantly need reassurance, they need their parents and siblings attention; a healthy child continuously seeks and receives love, comfort, assurance and happiness. Technology does not provide this on its own, it is a very useful tool but no substitute for parent-child interaction.

Games Addiction

Many Muslim parents leave their children to play, read, draw, study and view online mediums upon their own smart tablets or PC, assuming no apparent danger; however there are 'invisible problems' and 'immediate risks' which children become exposed to. Many become addicted because of the interactive cinematic experience of online video games and then begin to display the same symptoms as drug or alcohol dependence: the urge to continue playing at all costs and at all times; withdrawal symptoms (mood swings, aggression, shaking and anxiety; animosity towards good deeds, people of Deen and seniority).

Until they are able to recommence their 'session' they remain in this state of agitation and turmoil because game designers and software writers use powerful psychological techniques and variable rates of reinforcement (in plain English, the dangling of a carrot) as rewards to lure and keep the gamer online. This is a very similar approach to that of fruit (slot or one-arm bandit) machines in casinos; where illusions (imagery/sounds) are employed to convince users it is their skills which will inevitably reap rewards. What the naive and addicted gambler fails to realise is the benefits which accrue are to the games operator at the players expense (almost 70% of profits made by casinos are made in this way). Similarly, video game manufacturer's make their profits by preying on the vulnerability and susceptibility of youngsters who easily become addicted, trapped and constantly await release of the next game (software) and a more expensive gaming platform (hardware).

Responsible & Controlled Internet Viewing

'O you who believe! Save yourselves and your families from a fire, the fuel of which is human beings and stones...'

(Glorious Qur'an, 66:6)

haykh Ashraf 'Ali Thānwi ☙ commented, 'Concord is present in pre-occupation; whether this be of a Deeni or permissible worldly nature. In all conditions, enterprise is better than inactivity. Experience shows that whenever a person remains unoccupied, Shaytan prevails over him and, amongst activities, the company of the pious is best...' Experienced tutors offer the following advise:

1. Parents should locate computers and similar online devices in the family communal or living room and not children's bedrooms. Internet activity and viewing is thereby supervised and monitored.

2. Except for those businesses and institutes which 'genuinely' require high-speed broadband speeds, Muslim homes have no need for ultra speed internet connections; these are primarily for playing online games and downloading of films. Countries which have the fastest broadband networks (e.g. South Korea) also have the highest number of video game addicts, problems and treatment centres.

3. Invest and install parental controls to a *Firewall* with password on all Internet accessible devices to provide some form of control and prevention to inappropriate websites for young viewers. Look out for tell-tale signs of misuse; constant viewing; regular deletion of viewing history in web browsers and search engines; clicking of the mouse whenever somebody walks into the room; an insistence on positioning the monitor away from general viewing; unnecessary and constant wearing of headphones.

4. Encourage children to discuss their work and take an active interest in their viewing activities and browser history. Let them know it is

not they you do not trust but the self (*nafs*); one's own plus that of juniors. Discuss the dangers and harms of online addiction and wasting time. Regularly outline the benefits of good deeds, good behaviour, study and halāl wealth creation.

5. Provide sensible alternatives: a large library of authentic kitabs and variety of books; writing, art & craft material; permissible educational toys & games (not using a dice or music); informative publications and multi-media formats; keep-fit equipment, etc.

6. Devices such as smart tablets (e.g. iPad) and smartphones should not be purchased for young children who should be shielded from all video games to prevent addiction from an early age.

7. There is no real need for any Muslim to have a social network presence or blog. Any and all accounts should be deleted. Email accounts for children should be monitored. Any Skype, Messenger or similar accounts should be family and not individual based.

8. Internet viewing should not be allowed at salāh, meal, pre-school and pre-maktab times for anybody. Set a good example; disengage from Internet viewing at least 25 minutes before salāh time to allow for ablution, preparation, travel to Masjid, Sunnah and optional prayers. Generally parents are very lax in this matter (view attendance at Masajids to collaborate this); yet expect children to be pious and well-behaved. We have to ensure the entire household becomes punctual, regular and conscious about salāh (with *Jama'at*) from infancy (at home). Establish an environment at home wherein all participate in communal activities; for example performing salāh together, praying the Qur'an after Fajr together; listening to Deeni programs; daily kitab taaleem sessions; meals; cleaning and housekeeping; DIY activities; keep-fit at home; etc.

෮෨ඏ

Chapter Five

Three Important Tasks for Home Reformation

by

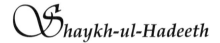haykh-ul-Hadeeth

Mawlana Muhammad Saleem Dhorat
hafizahullah

Reviewed

by

Mawlana Maseehullah Patel,
Mawlana Qãri Muhammad 'Abdullah

Salat and Salams upon the Final Messenger ﷺ

Allah ﷻ mentions in the Glorious Qur'an:

> *'Whoever, practices righteous deeds, whether male or female, while he/she has Imaan, then assuredly, We shall grant him/her a wholesome (i.e. peaceful and honourable) life. And We shall certainly reward them (the pious ones) in return for their righteous deeds.' (Glorious Quran, 14:97)*

Respected Brothers and Sisters, on this occasion it is my heartfelt wish to relate three important and clear issues; the acting upon which, by all of us, would result *insha'Allah* in success for ourselves and our children.

Firstly, every Muslim should vouch to ensure no possible disobedience to the Commands of Allah ﷻ will take place in the four walls of our homes.

We do not have control over our neighbourhood, our city, our country or even our street. Events have now transpired where we do not even have control over our own household; parents no longer have control over their children. Even the special and lofty relationship which existed between teacher and student no longer remains; during my childhood we witnessed Muslim students respecting their non-Muslim teachers. Why? Because, they are our teachers; who have taught us the alphabet, mathematics, science, geography, etc., etc.

The great scholar and jurist (*faqeeh*) Imam Aboo Haneefah ﷺ, who spent his entire life in researching Deeni Commands (*Masa'eel*), was observed respecting a janitor (*bhangee*); allowing him to proceed whenever they passed each other on the streets. When asked why he showed such respect to a *bhangee* akin to an elder; the Great Imam ﷺ replied,

'He too is my teacher, this is why I respect him; I have learnt a topic from him. Whilst researching a *mas'alah* it became necessary to ascertain when a dog attains puberty (*buloogh*)? Somebody suggested I inquire from the *bhangee*; therefore I approached him with this query. He informed me, 'When a dog raises his leg to urinate then understand him to be mature; until he does not do this to urinate, he is not *baaligh*.' This was no intricate matter of the Sharee'ah, rather it was a point of observation and experience, which because it was of benefit, the Great Imam ﷺ felt it necessary to revere this *bhangee* and regard him with the same esteem as a teacher.

Whither is the respect for parents and elders in this era?

When there is no total control over one's own children how may we hope to reform the entire neighbourhood, town or country? It is a very difficult task. This is no call for despondency; if a group of people endeavour with sincerity, then Allah ﷻ does create blessings to some extent or the other; however, what I would like to remind our ladies especially is the convention to not allow any disobedience to Allah ﷻ in our own homes; not by people who live therein nor by those who visit. Make a firm resolution, when such a motion is put into place, Allah ﷻ will show us the way. If the need arises consult (*ruju'*) the Scholars, Muftis and those professionals who are experts and experienced in this field.

Dialogue Between Sayyidduna Moosa ﷺ & Fir'own

Remember, fighting and disputing does not produce results...

'Invite (people) to the way of your Lord with wisdom and good counsel. And contest with them in the best of manner...' (Glorious Quran, 16:125)

Always conduct yourself with decorum and composure no matter how offensive and ill-mannered the other person may be. When Sayyidduna Moosa ﷺ was instructed to enter the Palace of Pharaoh (*Fir'own*) as a Messenger of the Creator of the Universe, Fir'own responded in an uncouth way;

'What is this Lord of the World?' (Glorious Qur'an, 26:23)

Whenever we introduce or inquire about an unknown person we refer to them as whom not as what; the latter is used when referring to an object. Obviously Fir'own's intention in using this phrase was to ridicule, denigrate and belittle the personality of Allah ﷻ in front of his courtiers in order to embarrass Sayyidduna Moosa ﷺ.

However Sayyidduna Moosa ﷺ was the repository of good conduct and understood the motive for this rudeness, 'If I respond in a similar ill -mannered way, all these people present will be deprived from guidance.' He therefore ignored the provocation, a common ploy of peddlers of falsehood (*baatil*) and resolutely stuck to his mission and purpose. Sayyidduna Moosa ﷺ maintained his composure and stature...

'He (Moosa ﷺ) said, 'Lord of the Heavens and Earth and whatever there is in-between; if you are to believe.' (Glorious Qur'an, 26:24)

Provocation

Today, the passion, concern and honour of Muslims is being provoked and instigated in a similar manner; that Islam teaches barbarity, aggression and terrorism. Various ploys are used; cartoons, novels, films, etc, etc, all designed to ignite Muslims to respond with animation. Muslim laity, uninformed of Deen, walking the streets are interviewed and cajoled into reactive and sentimental statements; which are then highlighted and advertised in newspapers, radio, TV and the Internet to give credence to the media's claims and present Muslims as uncivilised and barbaric.

This is nothing new; Fir'own also used a similar ploy to whip up support from his courtiers; however Sayyidduna Moosa ﷺ did not react emotionally, he responded intelligently, positively and with conviction,

> *'He (Fir'own) said to those around him, 'Are you not hearing?*
> *He (Moosa ﷺ) replied, 'Your Lord and the Lord of your early*
> *forefathers.' (Glorious Qur'an, 26:25-26)*

Not to be outdone, Fir'own retorted,

> *'He (Fir'own) said, 'Your messenger who is sent to you is a*
> *mad man indeed.' (Glorious Qur'an, 26:27)*

Sayyidduna Moosa ﷺ remained firm and focussed during the debate; not allowing Fir'own to detract and mislead; one should remain true to one's goal and purpose,

> *'He (Moosa) replied, 'Lord of the East and West and whatever*
> *lies between them, if you are to understand.' (Glorious Qur'an,*
> *26:28)*

Notice the message and methodology of the Prophet, total and faultless glorification of the Creator,

> *'Lord of the Heavens and Earth and whatever there is in-*
> *between...Your Lord and the Lord of your early*
> *forefathers...Lord of the East and West and whatever lies*
> *between them, if you are to understand.' (Glorious Qur'an, 26)*

All three verses show the high degree of recognition of *Ma'arifat* (recognition of Allah ﷻ) of Sayyidduna Moosa ﷺ, for he could have used other metaphors; Lord of the Sun; Lord of the Oceans and Lands; however he chose such eloquent terms to convey perfect and total Sovereignty of the Creator over all issues of the universe (place) and over all time (era),

'Lord of the Heavens and Earth and whatever there is in-between,'

All matter between time and place fall under Allah's ﷻ Dominion as do all affairs between sunrise (East), zenith and sunset (West); symbolically also meaning a person's birth, maturity and passing-away all fall under Allah's ﷻ Control. Generally, one person's fame commences from anonymity to eminence to gradual ignominy whilst another person grovels in disgrace, falls further into humiliation before Allah ﷻ grants blessings and anoints with honour. Likewise, many businesses commence from austerity, progressing to unthinkable riches before returning to paucity; whilst others flounder for long in poverty before Allah ﷻ grants blessings and dearth disappears to be replaced by assets.

Wise Conduct

The purpose of relating such realities is to highlight the need to call towards Deen with beautiful conduct and wisdom. Matters should improve not deteriorate; progress not regress; because the person whom you are trying to call towards Deen is uninitiated; you have understood through the Favour (*fadhl*) of Allah ﷻ that it is suicidal to keep a TV in the home; you have understood music and lack of purdah as destructive and all such matters as sinful and leading unto Hell; however the other person has yet to understand, this is why they are submerged in such sins. Concern and compassion together with inclination and hope upon only Allah ﷻ should be present; plea to Him, 'O Allah! You have full control over hearts; grant my spouse and children correct understanding and guidance.'

Adopt a beautiful wise approach, do not keep nagging and reprimanding, do not keep discussing one topic; choose the time and occasion and convey with affection. Everybody should vouch to ensure no possible disobedience to the Commands of Allah ﷻ will take place in the four walls of our homes; neither by our spouse, our children, our parents, our in-laws nor any visitor to the house. Those who have a habit of backbiting (*gheebah*) should stop this vile habit before entering; those who do not perform salāh should either not come into our home's at salāh time or will have to perform upon arrival; create such a environment wherein the entire household perform salāh on time, accordingly whenever a visitor does arrive who is lax, they will of a surety have to follow suit, perform ablution and pray. They will either come with the intention of praying or not come at all.

Advantages of Kitaab Study

Shaykh Qāri Siddeeq Bandawi ☙ related how one of his associates, a Scholar was teaching in a distant Darul Uloom. He was living alone in quarters provided for Staff and on many an occasion fellow lecturers would visit and pass a lot of time in idle chit-chat which would eventually lead to backbiting. This associate, out of courtesy, lack of courage and a mild-manner was embarrassed to rebuke his fellow scholars; he therefore wrote to his Shaykh and requested a stratagem to prevent this participation in *gheebah*. Qāri Siddeeq Bandawi ☙ suggested, 'Daily keep a kitab nearby with some episode or beneficial and interesting point marked. When your companions arrive, after exchanging formalities for a few minutes, mention how you came across this interesting episode and how you would like to relate it to them so everybody may benefit; commence reading and notice how these futile gatherings soon come to an end.'

After a few days of commencing this *taleem*, these *majaalis* of futility soon ended. No arguments or disputes; friendship still remains, one is still able to meet one's acquaintances, however the backbiting and slander no longer takes place.

First Task - Home Environment

People who have concern for the Hereafter (*Akhirah*) make *ruju* towards the *Mashā'ikh* and acting upon their instructions achieve success both here and in the *Akhirah*. Firstly, slowly but surely make such an environment within the four walls of our homes, wherein there is no disobedience to Allah ﷻ and every member of our household is punctual with salāh, zakat, sawm, hajj, honesty, in purdah, etc., etc. Moreover, visitors to the house must also not carry out any act of disobedience whilst within our home.

Second Task - Pious Household

Secondly, the members of our household must become so pious and Deeni conscious that they do not carry out any disobedience to Allah ﷻ even when outside the home environment. Make such effort and attention upon our spouse, children, parents, in-laws that just as they do not entertain *gheebah* within the home, similar is their distaste for this sin when outside. Just as they do not listen to music or view films within the home, similarly they should not carry out such activities outside. Just as they do not miss salāh at home, similar should be the case when outside. Just as they do not bring bad company to the home, similarly they should not associate with bad company when outside.

Should everybody take up this responsibility then every household will become reformed. However, our weakness is we do not make this our goal; we have concern for all other affairs of the world; we sit and talk about all others; about every other household; but no time or concern to self-assess. The final King of the Moghal Empire, Bahadur Shah Zafar ﷺ (1775-1862), an accomplished poet relates,

> 'When we were unaware of our own condition; we remained viewing other's faults and rendition; When gaze did truly fall upon one's trepidation; remained nobody in this world in a worse situation.'

Adopt wisdom and good counsel otherwise turmoil will result between parents, children, husband and wife. Children should be corrected from the moment they begin to disobey Allah ﷻ; from childhood they should be supervised, nurtured and not allowed to remain free. If two children are present and one snatches the other's share, instantly correct him. Do not consider it insignificant or amusing; immediately reform him; sit him down and affectionately make him understand his error and instruct him to make amends even offering a reward or treat. 'This is your brother's, return it to him and I will give you more in return.'

Training (tarbiyyah) of Children

When children misbehave, lie or bully somebody, we have a tendency to overlook, ignore and at times find it hilarious, considering them to be too young and funny. Whereas this lying, snatching, stealing and bullying will eventually become a habit leading to disastrous consequences.

There was a habitual thief who was caught on several occasions. Despite being punished each time, he would not stop stealing. Finally, the Judiciary concluded him to be a serial thief and passed the death penalty. Awaiting hanging in the gallows, when asked his final wish he requested a private meeting with his mother, who arrived at the prison in a state of despair. He reiterated his wish to say something to her in confidence and as she placed her ear to his mouth, he bit her violently and tore her ear off. In agony she cried out and all those nearby rushed to pull him away and scolded the thief, 'Scoundrel! Even at time of death, you commit an act of treachery!' He replied, 'Instead of reprimanding me, ask why I carried out this dastardly deed? Today I am being hanged because of my mother, why? Because when as a small child I used to steal small items such as eggs from the neighbourhood, instead of reprimanding she used to take the eggs and cook them for all of us. Had she stopped me then I would never have become a habitual thief. It is my mother who raised me thus; this is why I considered it appropriate to award her some punishment as well.'

We do not have true concern for correct upbringing (*tarbiyyah*); this is why we allow them to 'grow with the wind.' We only have concern when the child does something against our wishes; now the child is ruined; until then it did not matter how many Commands of Allah ﷻ were being broken or ignored; from infancy until late teens he or she missed salāh, but it does not matter; he is still very good because although he disobeys Allah ﷻ he obeys us.

The day this child decides to marry against his parents' wishes, notice the immediate change and damnation. Now he has become corrupted! Corrupted! He became corrupted from the time he began to disobey Allah ﷻ; when he spent his youth in the disobedience of Allah ﷻ; if he now begins to disobey you what is the surprise?

Children & Importance of Salāh

When a child does not pray salāh he is not thought of as disobedient, yes the day he begins to talk of marrying a girl whom we do not approve of, now he has become irreligious! Why? Because when a child does not pray salāh, in our society (*mu'āsharah*) our honour is unaffected. However, if the same child is observed with an 'outside' girl, our honour and the honour of our clan will be stained; now the boy has become disobedient to the Sharee'ah; whereas the missing of salāh and associating with a non-mahram girl are both major sins (*kabair*).

In the final analysis, the first item to be quizzed about on the Day of Qiyamah will be salāh; and a characteristic of salāh is prevention from acts of wickedness and depravity...

> '...*Surely Salāh restrains one from shameful and evil acts. Indeed remembrance of Allah is the greatest of all things. Allah knows what you do.' (Glorious Quran, 29:45)*

Whosoever is punctual and conscious of salāh is saved from immodesty (*be hayai*). When Sayyidduna 'Umar Farooq ✺ wrote a letter to his Governors, he mentioned, 'In my estimation the most important act is salāh, and therefore you should be punctual...'

Any person in power when writing to his ministers discusses the art of good governance; yet here we find Sayyidduna 'Umar ✺ reminding them of salāh. Why? He continues, 'Whosoever guards his salāh will guard matters of governance and importance to a greater extent.' These are the blessings of salāh.

Children & Importance of Mother Tongue

This is why we should be conscious regarding the *tarbiyyah* (Denni upbringing) of our children. If they address an elder as 'you,' correct them affectionately. We too should address them with respect, in this way the entire household will speak politely. Any inappropriate terms of address or speaking should be corrected, not with laughter or by slapping but by discussing with them the error and by showing the correct mode of speaking.

A few years ago, my young niece and nephew came to visit and they came into the library where I was studying. They were eating a packet of crisps my respected mother had given them. My niece asked, 'Uncle would you like some?' Immediately, I sat her down and instructed, 'We do not say this, rather we say, 'Uncle take some.'

Language is the Product of Culture

The difference may appear subtle or even pedantic, but the first is an act of modern courtesy; whilst the second is the Muslim code of hospitality. The first is formal, 'Would you like a cup of tea?' The second implies the warmth of human generosity and welcome, 'What will you drink, tea, coffee or something cold?' Notice the difference; this is why our *Akābireen* placed great importance in protecting our own language because any language is a product of its culture. If there is no esteem in the language from where will respect come from? The esteem present in Arabic is not present in *Farsi* (Persian) or Urdu; therefore when you observe the Arab's speaking amongst themselves, one is struck by the degree of respect. No matter how educated, wealthy, accomplished, powerful and influential the Arab child and no matter how ignorant or old the Arab father, it is not possible for both to be present in one place and the son be seated in a seat or position considered higher or better than the father. Even if the old uneducated father was to walk into the executive boardroom where his son is chairing a meeting with directors, immediately the son will rise from his seat and motion his father to sit in his place.

Even today in Arabia, where overseas labour is used to carry out menial domestic chores such as cleaning, cooking, chauffeuring, etc., etc, when the time comes to pushing the wheelchair wherein sits the father, it will be the son and not chauffer who carries out this act of service and good fortune. The chauffer will walk behind.

In Muslim culture, the name of the father, mother, ustadh or shaykh is not spoken, instead titles of honour and respect are used. This is why it is so important to preserve our mother language, for it heralds and safeguards respect within our homes.

Returning to the incident with my young niece, I made her understand, we Muslims do not ask, 'Will you have some?' Rather we say, 'Take some,' even if they decline we encourage, 'Eat some even if it be a small amount.' This is the unique beauty of Muslim hospitality. Now notice the effects of affectionately instructing our children. My niece thereafter went into the living room where her brother was also eating some crisps, as soon as I walked in, he too offered some to me, 'Uncle would you like some?' Immediately, my niece corrected him, 'We do not say this; we say Uncle take some.' This is the age of *tarbiyyah* (training);

wherein Muslim values, habits and character (*akhlaaq*) are highlighted, developed and ingrained. Our problem is negligence and a failure to place great importance and attention to the *tarbiyyah* of our children.

Concern For Household

Therefore, the first responsibility is to ensure no wrongful act takes place within the confines of our homes. If the husband is neglectful of *salāh*, there should be a pain in the heart, 'My husband is neglectful of *salāh*!' If films are being viewed, a pain should be present, 'O dear, a film is being viewed in our home!'

When a pain is present in the heart, then instinctively a *du'a* will emerge, moreover after this heartfelt *du'a* whatever admonition (*naseehat*) is made, Allah ﷻ will create the desired effect. Prophet Muhammad ﷺ narrated,

> *'Allah is very pleased with the husband who awakes his wife for tahajjud or fajr salāh and Allah is very pleased with the wife who awakens her husband for tahajjud or fajr salāh...'* (*Aboo Dawood: 1308*)

Our objective in life should be success for our spouse and close one's in this world and the Hereafter. We should make every effort to improve each other; let your spouse know of your affection and concern for them and this is the reason behind your encouragement to enact good and refrain from evil. You desire to see your spouse with you in Jannah. If necessary consult experts (pious 'Ulama and Mashā'ikh) as to how these issues and improvement to the home environment may be made. There should be no disobedience to Allah ﷻ by anybody coming to our home, nor should anybody from our household commit transgression outside also.

Third Task - Total Abstention From All Haram

The third important task is to ensure no impermissible (*haram*) wealth, material or foodstuff enters our household. Only permissible (*halāl*) items must appear, in this aspect our mothers, sisters and daughters have the greatest influence. They should advocate and encourage contentment (*qana'at*); be ready for the furniture, furnishings, clothing and foodstuff which the salaries of your menfolk is able to support. Everything should be halāl; whatever enters the throat should be halāl; whatever is worn should be halāl; furnishings should be halāl; car should be halāl; etc, etc.

We have a strange phenomena, when we shop we scrutinise the ingredients to make sure everything is halāl and so we should, however the income? Is this halāl or haram? Halāl ingredients purchased with haram money transforms the whole item haram. Similarly, if the house, furniture, carpets, appliances and car are purchased with haram finances, mortgages and agreements, then we are living, walking, sitting and travelling on haram. Address these issues; our income and expenditure must be halāl; this becomes easy when simplicity and contentment is advocated.

If a haram morsel enters the stomach, the ability (*tawfeeq*) to carry good deeds is not granted. Qāri Muhammad Tayyib ﷺ used to say, 'Allah ﷻ snatches away the *tawfeeq* to do good from the person who consumes haram.' Such a person is aware and even wishes to perform good deeds; however he lacks courage and will-power. Such a person observes all others reciting and praying; yet he sits idly unable to perform. Qāri Muhammad Tayyib ﷺ used to thereafter relate the couplet of Mirza Ghalib ﷺ (1797-1869),

> *'Am aware of the reward of worship, abstinence and all such;*
> *However my self refuses to act as much.'*

If these three tasks are implemented by all members of our households, then our entire community and society (*Mu'asharat*) will become reformed. If we were to deprive our child from basic arithmetic and then sit him in a test wherein he is asked to multiply 7 x 3, he will be totally clueless. Similarly, if we deprive our household from basic knowledge, understanding and awareness of Deen and then expect our children to perform the five daily salāh under threat of rebuke or force; then obviously this is folly, why? Because you never provided the training. This should be commenced from infancy and even if you have neglected; make an immediate start, however if you have become Deeni conscious now, do not expect your children to become cognisant overnight. If you try to use coercive force, within a week to ten days your relationship with your children is terminated; each refuses to look or talk to each other. Now the children rebel and make a point of undertaking such deeds which angers parents. Therefore, act affectionately and maintain dialogue and rapport; only raise subjects on appropriate occasions, make du'a for them. Take them unto the gatherings and company of pious scholars. Relate the episodes of the pious to them; for when this takes place the Mercy of Allah ﷻ descends. Certain Shuyook have stated,

> '*The Mercy of Allah ﷻ descends upon those occasions when mention is made of His pious servants.*'

Ponder, when these are the effects when their mention is made, how much greater benefit must be derived when sitting in their company.

May Allah ﷻ grant all of us *tawfeeq* and make our households pious (*saleh*) and happy, both from a Deeni and worldly perspective; and make our homes a venue for piety, blessings, mercy, angels and a place from where shaytan and the evil flee.

Shaykh Ashraf 'Ali Thãnwi ☙ narrated,

'In this era I consider the company of the Ahl-ul-Allah (pious scholars) to be compulsory (fardh-e-'ain) and issue a decree (fatwah) accordingly. What doubt is there in the religious compulsion of establishing a correct relationship with the pious in this day and age? Experience shows that nowadays the well-being of our Imaan is only possible in the company of the pious...and after establishing a correct relationship with them; through the Fadhl of Allah ☙ no magic (or media/temporal wizardry) can effect one.'

Shaykh Maseehullah Khan ☙ narrated,

'I am more concerned with good company than know-how and this is a concept fast disappearing; for there are only a handful of outstanding pious Mashã'ikh still alive and soon you will have to search for them and nobody will be available. Even those alive, are not held in the reverence they deserve, because their respect and standing is being eroded...Our pious elders have advised,

'Irrespective of whether one finds good company or not at least save oneself from the company of immoral people: then inshã'Allah you will remain pious for a person does not become corrupted himself; rather he deviates because of the company of others...'

Chapter Six

Tranquil Eye & Tranquil Company

Based Upon the Works

of

Shaykh Mufti Mahmood Hasan Gangohi 📿

Shaykh Ashraf 'Ali Thānwi 📿

Shaykh Hakeem Muhammad Akhtar hafizahullah

A short while in the company of the pious is better than a century of worship with sincerity and abstinence. Even in this era, numerous are the cases of people immersed in major sins, who after having adopted tranquil company of the pious, gave up a lifetime of bad habits permanently, very quickly, with the utmost of ease and minimum effort. This is the major benefit of associating with pious Scholars, Masha'ikh, Madrasahs, Khanqahs and Tableegh Jama'at; the greatest beneficiary is to one's self.

$\mathcal{A}$llah mentions in the Glorious Qur'an:

'O Believers! Fear Allah and join the company of the truthful.'

$\mathcal{O}\mathcal{S}$ ayyidduna Hanzalah Al-Usayyidi 爨 who was one of the scribes of Prophet Muhammad 爨, reported,

'I met Abu Bakr 爨 *who asked, 'How are you O Hanzalah?' I replied, 'Hanzalah has become a hypocrite.' He exclaimed, 'Subhānallah! what are you saying?' I replied, 'When we are in the company of Prophet Muhammad* 爨, *he reminds us of Paradise and Hell, we feel as if we are seeing them with our very eyes, and when we are away from Prophet Muhammad* 爨; *we attend to our wives, our children, our business, most of these things slip our minds.' Abu Bakr* 爨 *said, 'By Allah, I also experience the same thing.' So Abu Bakr* 爨 *and I went to Prophet Muhammad* 爨 *and I asked, 'O Messenger of Allah* 爨, *Hanzalah has become a hypocrite.' Prophet Muhammad* 爨 *said, 'What has happened to you?' I said, 'O Messenger of Allah* 爨, *when we are in your company, and are reminded of Paradise and Hell, we feel as if we are seeing them with our own eyes, but when we go away from you and attend to our wives, children and business, much of these things go out of our minds.' Prophet Muhammad* 爨 *replied, 'By Him in Whose Hands is my life, if your state of mind remains the same as it is in my presence and you are always busy in remembrance (of Allah), the angels will shake hands with you in your beds and upon your roads; but Hanzalah, time should be devoted (to the worldly affairs) and time should be devoted (to prayer).' He (the Prophet* 爨) *said this thrice.' (Muslim)*

haykh Mufti Mahmood Hasan Gangohi ☙ narrates, 'Undoubtedly in this world a human is affected by the environment around him. His state of heart and mind are constantly changing; accordingly he is in vital need of the company of a Shaykh and ambience of (the Masjid, Madrassah and Khanqah). Instead of the polluting, neglectful and unIslāmic atmospheres of school, college, office, shops and factories, in Deeni institutions; salāh, recitation of the Glorious Qur'ān, learning, remembrance and glorification of Allah ☙ and Durood are performed and salvation is achieved from the mischief of one's self (*nafs*): and the cohorts of Shaytan who flee from the company of pious scholars and *Mashā'ikh*.

Shaykh 'Abdul-Qādir Raipoori ☙ used to say, 'When the great Shaykh 'Abdur-Raheem ☙ was alive in Raipoor, his *Majlis* used to take place between 8 to 9 am wherein all students would emerge from their rooms to gather. Once whilst Shaykh 'Abdur-Raheem ☙ was sitting in the *Majlis*, his gaze fell upon the arriving Shah Allah'Baksh ☙ and he exclaimed, 'Come sit here.' The latter went and sat down. Later, a confidante inquired, 'Shah! What was it, why were you summoned?' He replied, 'What to say? I arose today at 2am and a voice was pounding away at my heart and mind...

'Undoubtedly, I am Allah! Undoubtedly, I am Allah!'

Many times I tried but the voice would not disappear. However as soon as the gaze of Shaykh 'Abdur-Raheem Raipoori ☙ fell upon me and he said, 'Come and sit here,' the voice vanished. Those trials, states, concepts and excellences which are not accomplished even after years of striving (*mujahadah*) are bestowed by Allah ☙ very quickly in the company of such souls.

Shaykh Anwar Shah Kashmiri ☙ once came to stay for some time in Lahore, where he had many students and associates. The poet Doctor

Iqbal was also resident here and some of his friends suggested he too should come with them to visit Shaykh Anwar Shah ﷺ. However, at the time he did not acquaint himself with scholars and therefore declined. One day, a close friend said to him, 'You have time to meet everybody here-there-everywhere throughout the world, what objection do you have in visiting him?' 'Okay, I shall come.'

Immediately upon arrival, the thoughts of Doctor Iqbal focused upon the hadeeth of Rasoolullah ﷺ wherein it is stated that all attendees to his *Majlis* used to sit with humility, reverence, tranquillity and attention in such a way as if birds were perched upon their heads and the slightest movement would cause them to fly away. The Companions ﷺ would not look hither thither but sit with veneration and serenity.

A similar atmosphere prevailed in the *Majlis* of Shaykh Anwar Shah Kashmiri ﷺ, wherein people posed intricate questions and received elaborate replies with references to various publications. This is why Shaykh Anwar Shah ﷺ was revered by his epithet 'Mobile Reference Library.' Impressed, Doctor Iqbal decided to attend the subsequent *Majlis* wherein infinity of the universe was mentioned. Shaykh Anwar Shah ﷺ recited one of his couplets...'*Final word on infinity of the universe...*'

Immediately, Doctor Iqbal, an acknowledged poet concluded, 'Oho, he appears to be a learned and well-read person.' Thereafter, he proceeded to ask some probing questions which Shaykh Anwar Shah ﷺ answered; whereupon he commented, 'This is what Isaac Newton has written.' Shaykh Anwar Shah ﷺ replied, 'Whatever Newton has written on this topic is from the works of 'Allamah Iraqi ﷺ without acknowledging it. This is fraud and plagiarism.' Doctor Iqbal inquired, 'Who is 'Allamah Iraqi and where are his publications?' Shaykh Anwar Shah ﷺ replied, 'I have a copy of his works present in Deoband.' (They were subsequently posted to Doctor Iqbal). Doctor Iqbal continued to ask and received replies to intricate questions. He was now convinced. When Shaykh Anwar Shah ۞ witnessed this acknowledgement, he commented, 'Doctor! I am not happy with you for your association with the imposter and charlatan Mirza Gulam Qadiani!' Immediately, Doctor Iqbal arose, returned to his residence, tendered his resignation as Secretary of the Qadiani Movement and repented for his error. He thereafter returned to the *Majlis* and said, 'Shaykh! The thorn which was an impediment has been removed.' Shaykh Anwar Shah ۞ focussed his gaze upon him and now a new spiritual world revealed and blossomed itself in the poet's heart...

> *'Able to alight dead hearts by spiritual radiance of theirs,*
>
> *O Allah what excellences You have filled in hearts of theirs?*
>
> *Rather than ask of the Pious, if you desire then go and observe them;*
>
> *for they have enlightenment rolled up in sleeves of theirs!*
>
> *If you long for spiritual progress, do service of theirs,*
>
> *for this wealth is unavailable from worldly people and wares.'*

Henceforth the direction and outlook of his poetry took a phenomenal change. Before he would write anything, now his prose took inspiration and direction from the works of 'Allamah Jalaluddeen Rumi ۞. His love for the personality of Rasoolullah ﷺ becomes evident in a couplet supplicating to Allah ﷻ...

> *'Cover this needy and destitute's failings on Day of Reckoning,*
>
> *accept my excuses and if You must make by beckoning,*
>
> *hide my sins from the gaze of Mustafa's ﷺ vision,*
>
> *O Hallowed and Autonomous Creator of all creation.'*

This transformation was due to the company of Shaykh Anwar Shah ۞.

Today, such company is neither valued nor considered necessary, hence our deprivation.

Shaykh Anwar Shah Kashmiri ﷺ himself was the repository of humility and respect. When Shaykh-ul-Hind Mahmoodul Hassan ﷺ returned from his incarceration in Malta, he used to hold a *Majlis* for Scholars after Fajr Salāh at his residence. 'Ilmi discussions amongst scholars would also take place and sometimes Shaykh-ul-Hind ﷺ joined in, however Shaykh Anwar Shah Kashmiri ﷺ maintained silence; sitting in utmost humility as if in salāh. After the gathering had left, Shaykh-ul-Hind ﷺ would ask, 'Anwar Shah! Do you wish to ask anything?' Whereupon, he would inquire, 'Shaykh, I wish to inquire about such-and-such hadeeth.' His full attention was towards his Shaykh, he never joined in any discussions or debate whilst in his presence nor initiated any questions.

When Shaykh-ul-Hind Mahmoodul Hassan ﷺ was about to be sent away from India and interned for a second time in Malta, he was asked who would be the Head Teacher at Darul Uloom Deoband. 'In the presence of Anwar Shah why is this question being raised?' The stature of Shaykh-ul-Hind ﷺ was such that one statement and the appointment of Shaykh Anwar Shah Kashmiri ﷺ was a formality and nobody dared oppose.

When the latter sat down to deliver his first lecture on Tirmizee Shareef, the introduction was read; however he was so overwhelmed with the impending departure of Shaykh-ul-Hind ﷺ that he could not continue. He closed the kitab and proceeded to the residence of Shaykh-ul-Hind ﷺ where he was sitting on his couch. Immediately, Shaykh Anwar Shah ﷺ rushed over and sat at the feet of Shaykh-ul-Hind ﷺ and began to sob holding his knees against his chest. The person who never spoke in the presence of Shaykh-ul-Hind ﷺ was now so informal and emotional. The latter stroked his hand over the head of Shaykh Anwar Shah ﷺ and said, 'Anwar Shah! My presence was a cause for many doubts arising; when I will not be here, the doubts too will not arise. And if a doubt should arise then Allah ﷻ will look after you. Go I entrust you to Allah ﷻ.' This reverence that was present in the hearts of juniors for elders and patrons has now vanished.

Shaykh Khaleel Ahmad ﷺ often travelled from Sahranpoor to Deoband to visit the numerous book shops and libraries to carry out research. If the library was closed he would acquire a key from the librarian and carry out his work. If there was a delay in having to wait for a train and time was available, he would visit associates. Once, after visiting the library, he arrived at the room of Shaykh Anwar Shah ﷺ who viewed him coming from a distance. Immediately, out of respect, the latter ran bare feet to welcome him, whereupon Shaykh Khaleel Ahmad ﷺ protested, 'Brother, what need is there for such formality, I was coming anyway?' Shaykh Anwar Shah ﷺ placed both his hands around the hand of Shaykh Khaleel Ahmad ﷺ and ushered him into the room. Those students already sitting inside were instructed to leave and a personal discussion took place before Shaykh Khaleel Ahmad ﷺ left to return to Saharanpoor.

Another Example

Shaykh Mufti Kifayatullah ﷺ had both studied and taught at Saharanpoor and was now resident in Gangoh; where he was an associate of Shaykh-ul-Hind ﷺ. During the time when the latter was incarcerated in Malta, a state of melancholy overcame Shaykh Mufti Kifayatullah ﷺ. Whilst performing *thikr* he was plagued by thoughts of suicide...he would pick up a knife...peer into a well, etc., etc. However, because he was a scholar, neither the knife nor the well could overcome him. Yet, such thoughts were besetting him and his Shaykh was in

Malta. He pondered hard about whom to turn towards...the name of Shaykh Khaleel Ahmad Sharanpoori ☙ struck a chord for he was amongst the foremost deputies of Shaykh Rasheed Ahmad Gangohi ☙. He wrote a letter seeking guidance from Shaykh Khaleel Ahmad ☙ who replied, 'Amazing that you should consider me fit for such an enormous task?' Perplexed as what to do now, Mufti Kifayatullah ☙ decided to pay a visit into the company of Shaykh Ashraf 'Ali Thānwi ☙ in Thāna Bhawan. He had to travel by train from Meerath to Saharanpoor en-route to Thāna Bhawan; however the train from Saharanpoor was delayed, he therefore came to Mazahir Uloom to meet Shaykh Khaleel Ahmad ☙ who embraced him. When in private, the latter inquired, 'What had you written? A scholar of your calibre writing and asking me...how could I be fit to guide?'

Mufti Kifayatullah ☙ replied, 'Shaykh if anybody were to say that you are not qualified then it would not be a criticism of you but of your mentor Shaykh Rasheed Ahmad Gangohi ☙ for having appointed you. Why did he choose you? Are the unqualified and incompetent ever appointed? Moreover, the Madrasah from where you have acquired education I too have been blessed with the opportunity of studying there, so I do have a claim upon you.'

Shaykh Khaleel Ahmad ☙ maintained silence and then remarked, 'Stay over.' After Esha salah, before he left for home he prescribed a slight decrease in the thikr program, 'Pray slightly loud upon the balcony of the guest room near my house so I am able to hear your voice.' Mufti Kifayatullah ☙ replied, 'Shaykh, I am unable to recite, allow me to leave it out and return to my teaching and lecturing.' Shaykh Khaleel Ahmad ☙ replied, 'Do not be perturbed, carry on with what you are doing, for a person once came to Shaykh Rasheed Ahmad Gangohi ☙ with a similar condition, he too was instructed in this manner.' This was related for the benefit of Mufti Kifayatullah 🌸 and to show authenticity of the approach. Thus he awoke during the latter part of the night and started reciting his thikr.

The practise of Shaykh Khaleel Ahmad 🌸 was to arrive at the Madrassah at beginning of Fajr time (*subah sadiq*) and remain in meditation until Fajr. After Fajr he inquired, 'How are you now?' Mufti Kifayatullah 🌸 replied, 'I feel at peace, the previous condition is no more.' 'Good, remain seated here outside my room,' so saying, Shaykh Khaleel Ahmad 🌸 entered his room. Mufti Kifayatullah 🌸 commented, 'I do not know what he was doing inside his room, but I could feel my wounded heart being massaged by Shaykh Khaleel Ahmad 🌸 and his stroking was causing blood and pus to come out. I was aghast for he was not visible...this experience lasted until *ishraq* (approximately half an hour after sunrise).' Thereafter he came out of his room and inquired, 'How do you feel now.' 'Completely at ease.' 'Okay come with me,' so saying he took me to his lecture on *Bukhāree Shareef*. Such luminance was visible in his lecture that Mufti Kifayatullah 🌸 desired the lecture never comes to an end and began to ask questions which were all answered. The lecture's of Shaykh Khaleel Ahmad 🌸 were noted for their brevity and clarity, yet the knowledge imparted was so deep as to be unattainable from kitabs. Such blessings and heavenly illumination was visible in the lecture which had not been witnessed by the visitor elsewhere and left him in a state hoping the program would carry on forever.

After the lecture, Mufti Kifayatullah 🌸 sought permission to go onto Thāna Bhawan which he was granted with instructions, 'On your return journey leave enough time to stay over for one more night; for some deficiency still remains.' Mufti Kifayatullah 🌸 thought, 'What is the discrepancy?' Accordingly, after visiting Thāna Bhawan he stayed over for two more days in Saharanpoor. As he sat down after Fajr Salāh outside the room of Shaykh Khaleel Ahmad ﷺ he felt as if his heart was being massaged again; but this time it was being filled with an entity which was providing strength and joy. In the first visit, illnesses were removed; in the second visit a tonic was given, whereupon Shaykh Khaleel Ahmad ﷺ commented, 'Now *inshā'Allah* there is peace and tranquillity, now you may go.'

This is the blessings of pious company (*suhbat*) and is not possible by self-study; for the Sahābah ﷺ sat in the company of Rasoolullah ﷺ; the Tābi'een ﷺ sat in the company of the Sahābah ﷺ; the Tabe Tābi'een ﷺ sat in the company of the Tābi'een ﷺ and so on, This is our chain of transmission.

Intricate and complex doubts are clarified whilst sitting in the company of the pious. Shaykh Ashraf 'Ali Thānwi ﷺ narrated, 'I used to go with certain scholastic doubts and uncertainties to the *Majlis* of Shaykh Rasheed Ahmad Gangohi ﷺ, however the need never arose to inquire, they were answered without asking. Sometimes the very question that was perplexing me would be posed by another attendee and Shaykh Rasheed Ahmad ﷺ would answer it; at other times he himself would address the issue and my reservations would be answered; occasionally he never said anything, nevertheless sitting in the *Majlis* was enough to dispel the doubt. I did pose one or two questions, whereupon he asked, 'Who is the questioner?' I replied, 'Ashraf Ali.' He did not tender any reply nor retorted, 'You seek an answer to such an obvious matter!' or 'Ask me some other time.' Rather he adopted complete silence, however this silence was enough to answer my queries in such a manner which would not have been possible had he lectured for hours..

Why? How? What is the secret? In reality, the original benefactor and benefit (*faidh*) is from Allah ﷻ Who inspires and bestows it upon the

Shaykh's heart; those sitting around him consequently profit as long as they have amiability (*munāsabat*) with him; confidence upon him and, no rancour in the heart towards him. If animosity is present, then no benefit will accrue, To gain benefit a clean heart is a prerequisite, for Allah ﷻ is the true benefactor whilst the Shaykh is a medium. When pure, clean and refreshing water falls from the Heavens upon a dome of marble it runs along the perimeter and down into a rain pipe. At the bottom outlet the rain water emerges and maybe employed...water hails from the sky and the rain pipe is an outlet...a necessary channel. Now if some person was to allow the outlet to accumulate with debris and rubbish, the water from the sky will still fall pure and clean but by the time it emerges from the channel it will be dirty and contaminated. This is the role of a Shaykh, a true and real Shaykh, whatever benefit (*faidh*) is bestowed upon him from Allah ﷻ is pure. However, if a student (*mureed*) does not have confidence upon him, is bitter towards him, is critical, nit-picking, judgmental and disparaging of his Shaykh's deeds, then the consequences will be witnessed upon his Shaykh's rapport. When disapproval (*takkadur*) settles in the Shaykh's heart, benefit stops.

An example is visible in hadeeth. Sayyiduna Hamzah ؓ, the Uncle of Rasoolullah ﷺ was brutally slain and mutilated in battle by Wahshi ؓ. When the latter accepted Islam at time of Liberation of Makkah (*fateh*) and pledged allegiance, Rasoolullah ﷺ advised Wahshi ؓ not to appear in his presence because viewing him would rekindle the pain of his Uncle Sayyiduna Hamzah's ؓ inhumane and sacrilegious death (inflicted by Wahshi ؓ), creating a natural aversion which would prove to be an impediment and barrier to spiritual benefit. However, he would receive *faidh* on account of his faith from wherever he may be.

It was the habit of hypocrites (*munafiqeen*) of Madeenah to forward complaints about the Sahābah ؓ to Rasoolullah ﷺ. He ﷺ addressed these *munafiqeen* not to bring such slanderous gossip of his Companions ﷺ for he desired to meet them with a clean heart free from any rancour or animosity. Similarly, pious *Mashā'ikh* themselves also desire there to be no resentment or bitterness towards any of their associates or *mureed* whereby the latter accrue maximum benefit. If there is dislike in either the Shaykh or *mureed's* heart, spiritual destruction will ensue. This is why there must be amiability between both parties, this will enable rapid progress and spiritual elevation.

Before senior *Mashā'ikh* used to be very influential and authoritative: this allowed them to overcome the weaknesses of the mureed's nafs similar to the physical way in which a strong wrestler overcomes a weakling. The Shaykh's spiritual strength and faculties would be used to overpower the wicked, bestial and shaytanic tendencies and habits of the *mureed* and spiritually extricate, reform and elevate him. However, if both the Shaykh and *mureed* are weaklings then Allah ﷻ have mercy upon them...for both are then indeed worthy of pity.

Shaykh Mufti Mahmood Hasan Gangohi ﷺ

Shaykh Mawlana Hakeem Akhtar hafizahullah narrates, 'Whatever deed or action is forbidden by the Sharee'ah is for our benefit. Every sin is harmful for the body. Show me a sin which is beneficial for you? We have been prohibited those deeds which are harmful for us, for example the viewing of non-mhram, why? Because if we become infatuated with them it is possible our spouse will become unappealing to us and we behave badly or oppress them. Today how many homes are broken? Those who protect their gaze, those who live a life of piety, their spouses live a life of unmatched bliss whilst those who are submerged in illicit viewing their character and habits become corrupted and their spouses and offspring suffer...'

Connection Between
Tranquil Eye & Tranquil Company

abee ﷺ commented,

'Solitude is better than evil companionship whilst the company of good is better than solitude.' (Baihaqee)

'The similitude of a pious companion is like that of a fragrance seller (whilst that of a wicked companion) is like that of a blacksmith. Accordingly, the fragrance seller will either give you some of his perfume or, even if he does not give, you will at least benefit from his fragrances. Whilst the blacksmith will either burn your clothes (if a spark or flame reaches you) or, if you are saved from this, then at the very least his smoke and odour will tarnish you.'

Shaykh Ashraf 'Ali Thānwi ﷺ narrates, 'Even if one does not derive complete benefit from good company some gain will be achieved, similarly even if you do not experience complete harm from bad company, some loss is sure to result. To associate with another is amazingly influential. No matter how weak a person, by associating with the right calibre and field of people, their expertise, competence, inclination, habits and character produces the desired effects. The company of nobles produces nobility whilst the company of evil produces wickedness. If a person associates with the scholars, he increases in intelligence; if he associates with the foolish, folly is created within him; if he stays amongst women, femininity results; if he stays amongst the brave, courage and valour are produced; if he stays amongst the lethargic, laziness arises. Whatever the nature of the company, their inclinations and outlook are sure to influence one. Whomsoever lacks courage to acquire and act upon Deen should endeavour to associate and sit with the pious People of Deen. Although these people are not Allah ﷻ, nevertheless they are not distanced or detached from Him either.'

Good Companionship ~ Mission of Prophets & Pious Scholars

Allah ﷻ created the Prophets and sent Divine Scriptures whereby the disoriented were guided, truth and falsehood were clarified. Whereas, one method would have been to only send Scriptures, wherein people could have read and acted upon the Commands of Allah ﷻ, but this never ever took place. Together with revelation of Divine Scripts Allah ﷻ sent the Prophets, this was the superior concept...good company:

'Whomsoever Allah takes into His employ,

He makes him/her from worldly pursuits unemployed.'

If a person does not possess academic knowledge, but he is fortunate to enjoy the companionship of pious scholars, then he will receive the necessary know-how. Yes, he will not be termed a Shaykh or Scholar, because this is dependent on academic lectures and learning, nevertheless he will be proficient in essential Islamic knowledge. Many of the Sahābah ؓ acquired their knowledge in this way, by association. Moreover, even true appreciation and understanding of academic knowledge is only possible by virtue of good company, this is why one handful of charity donated by a Sahābee ؓ is greater to a mountain size donation of ours, because they enjoyed the companionship of Rasoolullah ﷺ.

Company of Pious ~ Alchemy For Practising Upon Deen

An allegorical meeting took place between an ant who desired to visit the Kabah in Makkah Shareef and was obviously unable to do so and a pigeon who offered to take it there. When next the ant opened its eyes, it was circling around the Kabah. Similarly, to practise in entirety upon Deen, it is necessary to associate with pious scholars...

'Even if your heart is obstinate and as coarse as sandstone;

company of pious will transform you into a gemstone.

A short time in the company of pious nobles;

is better than a century of worship and a billion roubles.

Without the attention of Allah ﷻ and His servants of piety;

even Book of Deeds of an Angel would become a sordid diary.'

This is why even *Ulāma Zāhir* (academic scholars) are in need of the *Ulāma Bātin* (pious scholars), because without the company of spiritual scholars, the Pleasure of Allah ﷻ and perfect allegiance and practise upon Deen is impossible. Shaykh Maseehullah Khan ﷻ used to say,

'The Ahl-e-Ilm (ulāma zāhir) are in need of the Ahl-e-Suhbat (ulāma bātin), whilst the latter are not in need of the Ahl-e-ilm.'

This is easily understood when one appreciates even in worldly professions and skills, proficiency (and permission to practise) is not possible without association. After studying for many years, one still needs to spend time in the company of a doctor, lawyer, solicitor, accountant, engineer and architect. Nobody becomes proficient by academic study only; books are available for all professions, nevertheless association with a qualified and competent person is still considered necessary. Similarly, spiritual proficiency (*tarbiyyah*) is not possible by mere academic learning or self-study, it is dependent upon company of the pious. Every person should endeavour to spend some time in such company: once a week, a few days a month or a few weeks in a year. Parents endeavour to take their families to resorts for vacations annually, however few if any, are concerned with taking their children with them into the company of pious.

Features of A Good Companion

'If the company of your Shaykh is not possible then an alternative is a pious companion; combine this with remembrance of Allah ﷻ (thikr) and studying aphorisms (malfoozat) of pious Scholars.'

Although many people appear religious, the pious servants of Allah ﷻ have certain features which testify to their sincerity:

1. When you associate with such a person instinctively your attention turns towards Allah ﷻ, His Rasool ﷺ and Deen. Without even speaking, his demeanour reminds you of the personality of Allah ﷻ and thoughts of repentance and good deeds arise.

2. He possesses necessary knowledge of Deen and has received spiritual training under the supervision of an authentic Shaykh.

3. He practises upon the *Shar'eeah* and does not openly violate it.

4. He is adamant in following the Sunnah of Rasoolullah ﷺ.

5. He is merciful upon associates yet stern upon principles; he harbours no personal gain or is avaricious of wealth in return.

6. After associating with such a person for a while one finds an aversion and dislike for those bad habits and deeds which may have been committed for years; they begin to disappear without much effort; especially the habit of lustful gazing and backbiting. Greater the confidence upon the pious, greater the benefit.

7. Peace, contentment and tranquillity (*sakeenah*) descends from Allah ﷻ upon your heart when associating with a pious person.

8. Sometimes, when the compassionate gaze, attention and heartfelt du'a of a pious scholar falls upon one; many mental, spiritual, emotional and physical issues afflicting a person either vanish immediately or become bearable through the Grace of Allah ﷻ. The heart, soul and mind are strengthened.

Recent Examples of Inclining Towards Pious Company

haykh Hakeem Akhtar *dāmat barakātuhum* relates, 'There was a famous poet by the name of Hafeez in Jaunpoor, addicted to alcohol. When he observed Shaykh Dr. 'Abdul Hayy 'Arifee ﷺ, he commented, 'Shaykh! You are a university post-graduate so how did you acquire this pointed hat (*topee*) and lengthy *kurta*...whereby great, great scholars are inclining and learning Deen from you? From where did you acquire this life?' Dr. 'Arifee ﷺ replied, 'I stayed in the company of Shaykh Ashraf 'Ali Thānwi ﷺ through whom Allah ﷻ blessed us with the bounty of Divine Love (*muhabbat*).' Hafeez Jaunpoori inquired, 'Can we also go there?' Dr. 'Arifee ﷺ replied, 'Yes, of course you should go to the *Khānqāh*...a spiritual hospital; it is there precisely for sinners and people who have erred, for patient's arrive at a hospital not the healthy ones.'

Hafeez Jaunpoori departed for *Thāna Bhāwan* with a beard growth of a few days. Upon arrival, he summoned the barber and clean-shaved his stubble and thereafter presented himself and requested Shaykh Thānwi ﷺ to accept his *bayh*. Shaykh Thānwi ﷺ inquired, 'Hafeez! I know you are poet 'laureate' (of All-India), but tell me, whatever you had you have shaved that off also...why is *this* the way to repent (*tawbah*)?' Hafeez Jaunpoori replied, 'Shaykh! You are Hakeemul Ummat whilst I am Mareedhul Ummat...and the patient should present his true state so that the doctor may cure him. From today, *Inshā'Allah* no blade will touch this face.'

After making *bayh* he departed. A year later, it so happened that Shaykh Thānwi ﷺ travelled to Jaunpoor, he observed an old-man with a long beard approaching him and inquired, 'Who is this?' Associates replied, 'this is the very Hafeez who came to meet you last year.' Shāh 'Abdul 'Ghanee Phoolpoori ﷺ used to say:

'Even if a person, because of weakness of deeds, does not become a Walee of Allah ﷻ immediately, nevertheless through the blessings of establishing a relationship with the pious, Allah ﷻ will endow such a person with His Muhabbat before death.'

Another example is that of Jighar Murādabādee, a life-long alcoholic. When Allah ﷻ granted him tawfeeq to repent, he approached Khawajah 'Azeez-ul-Hasan Majzoob ﷺ, 'I wish to stop drinking and become pious...but how?' 'The same way we did!' replied the latter, 'We are a tax and revenue inspector, but look at our *kurta* and *izar*, our *salah* and *sawm*. You too go to a *Khanqah!'*

Jighar Murādee confided, 'Yes, I shall go but I am an alcoholic so I shall have to drink there also.' Khawajah Majzoob ﷺ related this predicament to Shaykh Thānwi ﷺ who replied, 'Khawajah, go tell him, I will not let him drink in the Khānqah! However, I shall make him a guest in my home because when Rasoolullah ﷺ hosted non-muslims in his house, then I may host a sinful Muslim.' Upon hearing this reply, Jighar Murādee began to weep, 'I always thought these pious Saints would hold a sinner with loathing and contempt, today I have realised there is no one more affectionate than them.' Thereafter, he requested four du'aa's from Shaykh Thānwi ﷺ: (1) To stop drinking alcohol. (2) To grow a full Sharee' beard. (3) To perform Hajj. (4) His death be upon Imān. Shaykh Thānwi ﷺ raised his hands and made du'aa.

Jighar Murādabādee ﷺ stopped drinking completely. He suffered withdrawal symptoms and fell dangerously ill. The doctors advised he drink a little...to which he replied, 'If I keep drinking I may live a few days longer but in the Wrath of Allah ﷻ, however if I die having stopped drinking I will greet death whilst in His Mercy.' He recovered, departed for Hajj and returned with a Sharee' beard.'

Chapter Seven

Immoral Gazing

& Fantasising

From 'Tasheelul Mawa'iz' of

$\mathcal{S}$haykh Ashraf 'Ali Thãnwi ⁕

With additional notes from the works of

$\mathcal{S}$haykh Mufti Muhammad Taqee Uthmãni

hafizahullah

$\mathcal{S}$haykh Qãri Muhammad Tayyib ⁕ *narrated, 'Marriage (Nikah) is the way (Sunnah) of the Prophets* ﷺ *and in Islam is not only limited to the category of transaction but is elevated to the level of worship (ibaadat). Prophet Muhammad* ﷺ *narrated,*

> **'Nikah is half of Deen; regarding the other half adopt taqwa (awareness and concern) for Allah** (﷽)**.'** *(Mishkāt)*

It is nikah which saves a person's chastity, modesty and is a means of keeping thoughts pure; a person is saved from impermissible (haram) and is contained within the parameters of permissibility (halāl). It is nikah which ensures family ties, unity, welfare and progress.'

'He knows the treachery of the eyes and whatever is concealed by hearts.' (Glorious Qur'an, 40:19)

Shaykh Ashraf 'Ali Thānwi ﷺ narrates, 'This is a Glorious Verse the words of, which are few, however the implication is enormous. In this Glorious Verse, Allah ﷻ has highlighted an illness of ours and the abhorrence thereof. Generally, people are sinking ever deeper into this illness, hence my preference in highlighting this disease from amongst the many spiritual illnesses which afflicts people; by sickness is implied sins.

Sickness is not as harmful as sins

Readers may be surprised and shocked to read a sin being described as an illness. Reality is just as sickness produces difficulty so does sinning; paradoxically the difficulty produced by transgression is infinitely greater to that experienced from a disease because the ultimate result of any illness is death and death in itself is an escape from many predicaments and therefore a blessing (for a Muslim). Whatever the illness; its effects are because of the relationship and connection of the soul to the physical body. For example, a person who suffers a stroke or who becomes paralysed does not feel any sensation in those limbs, which are paralysed or affected by the stroke. Even the application of countless needles or injections in the affected areas are not felt; because the previous relationship of the soul to these areas has been compromised if not totally severed; these limbs are still being nourished otherwise they would putrefy like a dead body. When such is the experience of a paralysed limb, one may understand the non-existence of pain (for a Muslim) when the soul is totally separated from its earthly realm.

Two states of freedom from illness

An adage comes to mind. A certain quack (incompetent physician) was once described as a person through whose diagnosis and treatment the illness did not remain...because the sick person did not remain. Similarly, an opium addict was lying in his den smoking when a fly repeatedly came and sat on his nose; unable to swat it away, finally in frustration he picked up a knife and sliced his nose off and commented, 'There no longer remains the portion for you to sit on.' This is one way of finding freedom from illness and predicaments; whereas the preferred way is to be cured and regain good health.

Episode of Sayyidduna Abu Talha ﷺ & Umm Sulaym ﷺ

In the final analysis, when a (Muslim) dies, then no illness remains; no pain, no cough, no cold, no worry nor any sorrow; all anxieties and hardships come to an end; complete comfort and peace. This brings an episode to mind. There is considerable praise mentioned in *hadeeth* regarding Sayyidduna Abu Talha ﷺ and his wife Umm Sulaym ﷺ. Once their young child (Umayr ﷺ) fell ill and Abu Talha ﷺ would come and inquire about him everyday upon return home. One day whilst he was away on a journey, the child passed away. Umm Sulaym ﷺ thought, 'If I inform his father now, he will neither eat, nor rest or sleep and nothing may be done now anyway; I will inform him later.' When Abu Talha ﷺ returned late at night, he inquired firstly about the child, Umm Sulaym ﷺ maintaining her composure and courage decided to act with wisdom; neither lying and thereby sinning nor blurting out the news of their child's death. Piety is such a concept, which exemplifies intelligence and understanding; accordingly Allah ﷻ blessed her with a beautiful response, 'He is resting in peace now.'

There is no greater peace than death (for a Muslim). Sayyidduna Ibn 'Abbas ﷺ narrates, 'When my father 'Abbas ﷺ passed away, a villager gave me such condolence which nobody else did. He said, 'You be patient and on account of your patience we too will become patient; because we are smaller and you are our elder; and the patience of juniors comes into effect after the patience of elders. By your father's death, you have suffered no loss but have gained because you have acquired reward and this reward is greater than 'Abbas ؓ; and your father 'Abbas ؓ has not suffered loss either; for he has reached Allah ﷻ and Allah ﷻ is better for 'Abbas ؓ than you.'

Death is a gift for a Mu'min

It appears in Hadeeth that 'Death is a gift for a Mu'min.' Whereas a human's constitution is such that he flees away from it; why? Because he has not observed the Hereafter. Death is like a train carriage, which transports a person from one place to another; from this world to the Hereafter. When a person boards a train, he is unaware of what awaits him at his destination; when he arrives there, he witnesses numerous trappings; a reception *par excellence*; countless items of food and drink, etc., etc. Only now does he realise, *Allahu Akbar*, there are great blessings for us here and what we left behind was so, so inferior. In fact, even the thought of this world does not arise.

Those pious personalities who have witnessed the Hereafter with their spiritual vision consider the trappings of this world as insignificant. This world in comparison to the Hereafter is like the realm of a mother's womb to planet Earth. Just like a baby does not happily arrive in this world, similarly a person does not wish to enter the Hereafter; just as an unborn child regards his mother's womb as everything until he experiences this world, similarly until we leave this world and experience the Hereafter we will always regard this world as everything.

Accordingly, death is a blessing and medium of peace and comfort (for a Muslim); this is why Umm Sulaym ؚ replied; 'He is resting in peace now.' Assured, Abu Talha ؚ sat down to eat with relish and thereafter expressed his desire to make love; which his wife consented to, whilst internally she must have experienced great turmoil and grief. After lovemaking Abu Talha ؚ slept whist his wife laid awake. After they had bathed, performed Fajr Salāh and Abu Talha ؚ had returned from the Masjid, Umm Sulaym ؚ posed a question, 'Tell me, if somebody borrows a trust (*amānah*) to us and then requests its return, do we return it happily or with grief and complaint?' 'Why, return it happily.' 'Well, Allah ؚ has recalled his trust (*amānah*), now you adopt patience.' Upset, Abu Talha ؚ replied, 'Why did you not inform me last night?' She replied, 'What benefit would it have made? You would have unnecessarily grieved.'

Illnesses of the soul are more severe than physical illnesses

The greatest repercussion of any physical illness is death and because death provides freedom (for a Muslim) from all difficulties, it is not as epic (as envisaged); nevertheless, our concern for physical sickness is unlimited. In contrast, spiritual illnesses, i.e. sins are dismissed as insignificant and unimportant; whereas they are so destructive as to suspend one between life and death; condemning the perpetrator to a stay in Hell. If death were to arrive there it would be a blessing, this is why we should be ever so concerned with spiritual ailments, however our condition is such that the slightest cough or fever and we visit our Doctor whereas for the hundreds of spiritual ailments that afflicts us we are unconcerned. Every sin is to be considered lethal and avoided but especially those sins, which we consider insignificant. Somebody asked Hippocrates (*Buqrāt*), 'Amongst illnesses which is the most severe and lethal?' He replied, 'The illness which you consider insignificant.' Similarly, the sin, which you consider irrelevant and minor, is the most destructive.

Immoral gazing & corrupted intention are considered insignificant

'He knows the treachery of the eyes and whatever is concealed

by hearts.' *(Glorious Qur'an, 40:19)*

In this Glorious Verse, mention is being made of two sins, which people consider trifling or minor; this is why I have chosen this Verse and; from the numerous sins connected to the eye and heart, the one's implied here are immoral gazing and incorrect intention. Although both are considered wrong, nevertheless they are not regarded as lethal and destructive as they should be. Observe, after committing either of these sins the least effect that should arise is staining of the heart; however no constriction is acknowledged because people dismiss these sins as trivial. Ogle at a non-mahram lady or a handsome boy, people think 'so what?' Just the same as staring at any other beautiful object; whereas this is a sin, which even the elderly, are submerged in. Not all are immersed in adultery; because this requires a willing partner, expense, circumstances, privacy and complete lack of shame, modesty and faithfulness. Many refrain due to the possibility of others finding out and ignominy; many because of acquiring some lethal sexually transmitted disease; many because of lack of resources; many because of their honour, especially those who have some connection to Deeni practise, they very rarely become entangled in adultery. However, almost all are submerged in immoral gazing and ogling; as this requires no resources nor is there any possibility of disgrace because only Allah ﷻ knows. If an educated or professional person ogles, he remains educated; no difference arises in his profession and no disgrace is suffered, nor does anybody generally become aware of the sin. All consider the elderly voyeurs living within our midst as friendly, social and polite with the ladies and affectionate towards youngsters. When sins of the eyes are not noticeable, how may sins of the heart be known?

Immoral gazing darkens the eyes

Pious scholars have written that immoral gazing produces such darkness in the eyes, which any person possessing true understanding and insight is able to discern. If two anonymous persons of identical age and appearance are present; with the 'only' (sic) difference between them being one of piety and impiety; then even a cursory look at the eyes of each will reveal to an astute observer how the eyes of the pious person will radiate with illumination whilst from the eyes of the sinner will exude a type of obscurity. Nevertheless, those pious scholars who do become aware of this do not humiliate or expose people; rather they conceal the perpetrators identity.

Shaykh 'Abdul-Qadir al-Jilani ﷺ

Once Shaykh 'Abdul-Qadir al-Jilani ﷺ was delivering a lecture on hadeeth in the Masjid, when a student arrived late. Through intuition (*kashf*), the lecturer realised the student was in need of obligatory bath (*ghusl-e-janabat*); Shaykh 'Abdul-Qadir al-Jilani ﷺ therefore halted him outside the Masjid and taking hold of a bathing apparel (*lungi*) addressed the class, 'Today I feel slightly tired, we shall proceed to bathe in the River Tigris and become refreshed.' Returning from this revitalising excursion, Shaykh 'Abdul-Qadir al-Jilani ﷺ commented, 'Let us not be deprived and study for a while.' Out of shame, the student was reduced to shivers however his integrity remained intact; such is the magnanimity of pious scholars; look at the kind and chivalrous manner in which he made the student perform *ghusl*. Accordingly, those who are fortunate to enter and benefit from their company; should therefore not attempt to hide their inner conditions because hiding one's spiritual shortcomings is due to one of two reasons; firstly, out of fear that by finding out he will consider us as wretched and inferior. Well, this is not possible, because a truly pious person only regards his own self (*nafs*) as the most contemptible. Secondly, due to concern that by finding out our faults they will reveal it to others; well this too is not possible in a truly pious person. Therefore, when there is a genuine intention to find cure for spiritual ailments, one should clearly relate spiritual conditions; otherwise without a valid reason one should never relates one's sins to another, for this in itself is a sin. Those pious scholars who do become aware of the sins of others do not reveal it and those who are slanderers and gossip mongers do not really get to know of the sins of others.

Immoral Gazing is easily enacted & generally starts in youth

Other major sins such as stealing, adultery, etc., require means, opportunities, strength and determination to carry them out; whereas immoral gazing requires no such resources; this is why even the old are immersed in this sordid vice. An old-aged person's legs are dangling in the grave, yet he still ogles. I met an old person who was Deeni conscious, who related his woe of how he was immersed in this illness of surreptitiously gazing at young boys; another old man had the habit of staring at women and he related how he had become infatuated with this practise since his youth. Most sins, like the habit of smoking, are committed in the vigour of youth; they then become habitual and remain until the time arrives to enter the grave. The difference between a young and old person immersed in the same illness is that the former will generally seek out a cure whilst the latter, out of shame, is reluctant to mention it to anybody; and because these sicknesses do not generally become known to anyone; they remain hidden and are even overlooked by one's self because they are dismissed as minor sins. This is precisely why Allah ﷻ highlights them:

'He knows the treachery of the eyes and whatever is concealed by hearts.' (Glorious Qur'an, 40:19)

Our thinking that nobody is aware of these misdeeds testifies to our lack of intelligence and understanding; whereas Allah ﷻ is so aware of your surreptitious behaviour that the danger of Divine Wrath descending upon you is imminent. When Allah ﷻ is aware and He ﷻ has full and complete control over you then you should be petrified. Ponder, people generally are of two kind; firstly, those who possess at least a modicum of integrity and honour and secondly; those who possess no such shame whatsoever. The first type, when they became aware that somebody may get to know of their sordid behaviour abstain totally there from; this awareness, sense of honour and the thought of another finding out is enough to stop them from sinning.

However, the second type, who lack any form of honour and shame; they are only scared of brute force and apprehension; they are being warned of impending punishment; this is the only language they appreciate and understand. Both types of people are warned; to be extremely conscious of these sins.

We should now self-assess and ascertain how much effort or thought we give to be saved from this sin. In my estimation, from amongst a thousand, maybe one person is saved from immoral viewing. Generally, people are submerged in this squalid sin, regarding it as extremely minor. Youngsters will acknowledge their misdemeanour whilst the older generation will interpret their lack of vigour as proof of lack of desires and an incorrect excuse to justify continuous involvement in this illness.

Difference in viewing beautiful people and beautiful objects

Some people labour under the false notion that viewing a beautiful person is the same as viewing a beautiful object such as a rose or dress. This is a completely wrong analogy. The desires, craving and longing which are produced in gazing at a beautiful (non-mahram) person and the joy which arises when observing an object of beauty, such as a car or building are totally different. When an exquisite dress or apparel is observed, the thought does not arise to embrace and kiss; however when a beautiful (non-mahram) person is viewed, such desires do arise. Desires in both cases are totally different; another misconception is when you hold your own child and you hug and kiss him or her; this is not the same as hugging somebody else's child. In the first, the biological and paternal feelings will not allow any carnal desires to take hold; whilst in the latter, such desires and thoughts do arise because the self (*nafs*) plots further afield. When a beloved separates, the pangs are different to when one's offspring becomes detached.

Although all forms of illegal gazing are sinful, nevertheless the practise of ogling at boys (*ephebophilia*) is lethal. Shaykh Abul Qasim Kashmiree ❀ narrates, 'Whosoever wishes to become pious, then for them to intermingle with women and young boys is extremely harmful and an impediment in his attempt to reach his goal.' Another Shaykh ❀ narrates, 'Whosoever Allah ﷻ wishes to eject from His ﷻ Court then He ﷻ allows such a person to incline and become afefectionate towards young boys.'

Even some women are submerged in illicit gazing

Another additional harm of immoral gazing, not present in other sins, is the ever-increasing submergence in voyeurism. All other sins have an eventual threshold; where sooner or later, the self (*nafs*) tires and loses interest; however the self's demand for immoral gazing increases the more one indulges in this sordid practise. Observe, a glutton will eat and eat, but eventually he will be able to eat no more. Similarly, a habitual drinker will drink and drink but then no more, however voyeurism is such a disgusting sin that the self is never satisfied; it is the pinnacle of all sins.

There are an increasing number of women who are involved in illicit gazing and who make an exhibition of themselves whereby men are able to view them. It appears in hadeeth:

'Allah ﷻ curses the ogling man and the ogled woman.' (Mishkaat)

Many women deliberately allow themselves to be viewed in an attempt to entice and beguile men; whilst many women who do adopt purdah, nevertheless live at home dressed as tramps; in front of their spouse they dress shabbily; however whenever the time arrives to travel away they dress to please. Even on family and social occasions (weddings, Eid, death, etc.,), when many women congregate together, they become immodest and will peep at the bridegroom and male attendees; whilst their men folk too will snoop into a room full of women.

Intermingling at social events

haykh Mufti Muhammad Taqi Uthmāni *hafizahullah* narrates, 'On occasions of weddings (and death), we are now beginning to witness such intermingling even amongst those considered religious which was unthinkable a short time ago. Those men who occupy the first row in the Masjid, those considered pious, even their womenfolk now dress in their finery and intermingle with non-mahram men; no vestige of purdah or modesty. Yes, the menfolk are still considered religiously conscious; their faces the paradigm of piety.'

Go past any gathering in a Muslim neighbourhood, it is difficult to fathom whether a wedding or funeral is taking place. There may be a vestige of separate seating and there may a few skull caps and long head scarves visible outside the home of the funeral (*janāzah*); but the banter will be the same; the intermingling will be the same; ladies will walk-in-and-out past a congregation of men folk fiddling their mobiles but the general atmosphere is identical. A huge hue-hah is made and *Kalimah Shahādah* recited loudly when the *janāzah* is carried in and out of the home of the deceased by men in front of non-mahram women who remain transfixed as if mannequins.

No attempt is being made to end or address these unIslamic practises; our elders and reformers have given up all hope; is it therefore any surprise we do not become submerged in turmoil, frustration and catastrophes? We are fortunate Allah ﷻ has not unleashed His Divine Wrath upon us because of the blessings of Rasoolullah ﷺ.

Remember, events have taken such a turn for the worse, that a truly Deeni conscious person has to decide on such occasions to take cognition of the Sharee'ah and abstain from such family gatherings. Let family members feel offended for they do not take your feelings into consideration. If you are purdah conscious and they invite you; what arrangements have they made for your purdah? When they do not take your purdah into consideration why are you taking their feelings into consideration? Who is insulting whom? Until a few determined ladies take a stand such gatherings will remain a conglomeration of sins albeit with a Deeni hue.

When family members of Shaykh Muhammad Idrees Khandhalvi ﷺ suggested he furnish his living room with sofas for the benefit of visitors, he replied, 'I have no longing for sofas nor do I find comfort thereupon; I feel comfortable on the carpet; I will remain working thereupon (he was one of the foremost scholars and prolific writers of his era). Why should I take into consideration the feelings of worldly people who come to meet me when these very people have not changed their lifestyle or deeds in anyway because of me? When they do not take me into consideration why should I take them into consideration?' He was not rude or obstinate, rather he was a very generous and hospitable person, however in terms of Deen, he remained firm upon the Sharee'ah.

Sometimes it does happen that separate quarters and arrangements are made for ladies in purdah; however even here perverts and 'peeping toms' will try to gate crash under some pretext.

Deeni conscious ladies should arise and unreservedly boot such voyeurs away, 'What are you men doing here? Woe betide, be off with you! We will not tolerate any non-mahram here!' Do not worry if somebody takes offence, after all family arguments and disputes occur over trivial issues at all weddings and funerals.

Until a few determined ladies and men do not take a stand, modesty will be compromised and no end to this scourge will appear. Either take a stand or await the Punishment of Allah ﷻ.'

Fantasizing

'He knows the treachery of the eyes and whatever is concealed

by hearts.' (Glorious Qur'an, 40:19)

Shaykh Ashraf 'Ali Thānwi ﷺ narrates, 'Allah ﷻ is well-aware of what people conceal in their minds and hearts; this is an even more lethal sin; for many a person fantasises about women and young boys in this manner; deriving pleasure in this way whilst still regarding themselves as religious and pious. This is a deceptive ploy of Shaytan, because many a times, by fantasizing, plotting and talking within the heart, greater harm and spiritual destruction arises. Why? Mutual physical attraction or relationship is many a times not possible and by fantasizing, the self has free play to conjure and derive unlimited psychological and egoistic pleasures; further entrenching thoughts about the person. To compound this sickness, the perpetrator regards him/her self to have achieved much by not physically viewing or talking to the object of fantasy despite desiring to do so; as if some great act of abstention (*mujahadah*) and purity; little understanding the fantasies they have enjoyed were also impermissible and devastating.

Accordingly, one should endeavour never to fixate the thought of anybody else; and this implies blocking all the faculties (ears, eyes, touch, smell and thought) from deliberately or negligently inclining towards those avenues prohibited by the Sharee'ah; venues and mediums of photography, lewd imagery, music, intermingling, etc., etc. There is also one major difference between immoral gazing and fantasising; nobody but nobody may become aware of the latter except Allah 🕮. There is always the possibility somebody may view a voyeur's act of gazing, ogling or peeping and take umbrage; but nobody except Allah 🕮 is aware of the fantasies a person plots in their heart. Therefore, only such a person will save themselves from fantasising who enjoys a strong and conscious bond, awareness and fear of Allah 🕮. There are stages or gradations in saving oneself from fantasising. The first stage is when the heart inordinately demands and; to oppose this unreasonable desire. The second stage is to weaken such heartfelt desires and thirdly, to completely remove craving in the heart for all such illegal desires.

First Stage – Easy Method of Preventing Fantasies

To prevent a thought from fixating in the heart is within one's control; whenever such a thought arises then use the strength of your mind to defer it; use the same faculty of thought to imagine a ugly person; for example, an extremely dark-skinned, short, lame, blind, deaf, stuttering, bald, wrinkled, crooked, goofy-tooth, thick lipped, runny nose person, shabbily dressed with flies encircling him. If Allah 🕮 wills, the harms that would have ensured by imagining your object of beauty will vanish. If after repeatedly adopting this method of contemplation, thoughts of the beauty still remain, then force yourself to understand how he or she will soon die; their body will be placed in a grave to wither, rot and become food for worms. However, this method of reflection will only prove beneficial if the intention really is to remove her thoughts from your heart; for this is a temporary measure.

Second Stage – Preventing Urge to Fantasise

To prevent further urge to fantasise in future, the only method is to remember Allah ﷻ in abundance. Secondly, also fixate the thought of His ﷻ Punishment. Thirdly, ponder how Allah ﷻ is aware and He ﷻ has full power over me. When one adopts these measures consistently over a period of time, then the dacoit lurking in the heart will *insha'Allah* one day leave; however it will take time, therefore do not be hasty, for such ingrained illnesses take more than a few days or weeks to be cured. Nevertheless do not forgo courage; slowly, slowly the urge will lessen and will come under your control.

Third Stage – Complete Annihilation of Immoral Desires

A third stage envisaged is where there no longer remains the medium which gives rise to such immoral thoughts and fantasies; wherein such a state is created that even the urge and desire does not arise. This is the thinking of those unintelligent Deeni conscious people who regard such a state as the goal and who become agitated and perplexed when this is not achieved. Whenever the urge to imagine or fantasise arises, they regard their efforts (of opposition and striving) to have been in vain; to the extent they utter such statements out of despondency, which are classified as disrespectful and inappropriate. This is a Shaytanic deception; this is not the objective, that no thought must ever arise; for if such thoughts and urges never occurred, what achievement would it be to have refrained oneself from sin? If a blind person claims, 'he has never ogled at anyone,' what is the big deal? If an impotent person claims, 'I do not approach women,' what is the feat? Accomplishment is despite being able to sin, but still managing to refrain there from.

In the final analysis, it really is a matter of great shame that we utter and claim to be lovers and devotees of Allah ﷻ yet our vision and attention is towards others. An episode comes to mind; a young maiden was walking out of the village on some errand, when a pervert began to follow her. Sensing mischief, the young maiden abruptly turned around and confronted the follower. 'Who are you and why are you following me?' The scoundrel replied, 'I have fallen in love with you, this is why I follow you.' The young maiden commented, 'Look yonder, comes my sister, younger and prettier than me...' As the rogue turned around to have a look, the young maiden kicked him and commented, 'Is this upon what you claim love?'

If we are made to stand before Allah ﷻ and He ﷻ was to ask us simply, 'Why did you turn away from Me and incline towards others?' What answer shall we be able to give?

This is no trivial or far-fetched philosophical matter; we need to prepare and bear them in mind.

Another tonic, which will reinforce the above instructions, is whenever the urge to sin or fantasise arises in the heart, make ablution and pray two rakaats *Salat Taubah* and make du'a.

For the first few days, no doubt you will have to pray quite a few rakaats; the next day the thoughts will appear much less and within a short while they will almost disappear all together because *salāh* is very difficult and burdensome upon the self (*nafs*). When it observes you praying upon the smallest deliberation, then such stray thoughts (*wasawis*) will *insha'Allah* disappear.

Now let us make du'a that Allah ﷻ saves all of us from such tribulations. Ameen

Chapter Eight

Harms & Cure for Evil Gazing & Illicit Relationships

$\mathcal{S}$haykh Hakeem Muhammad Akhtar

hafizahullah

'To antagonists He bestows perishable pleasures,
to friends He endows pangs of heartfelt treasures,
the former find waves upon a calm shore,
whilst I acquire tranquillity even in uproar.'

Salāt and Salāms upon the Final Messenger ﷺ

Ŝhaykh Hakeem Muhammad Akhtar *hafizahullah* relates, 'In this era, amongst means of destruction for the people of Deen, devoutness and piety; homosexual relationships are more lethal than illicit heterosexual behaviour. Moreover, because there are fewer impediments in homosexual conduct, Shaytan quickly embroils the self (*nafs*) in this sin, whereas heterosexual behaviour towards unlawful women is generally restricted to amorous gazing. Shaykh Ashraf 'Ali Thānwi ﷺ narrated:

1. *The harms and destruction which are caused by viewing, talking, flirting and associating alluringly with unlawful women and young boys in privacy are so severe and catastrophic that it is impossible for me to express them in words.*

2. *Unlawful love is a form of Divine Chastisement; akin to the existence between life and death which people of Hell will experience...*

ثُمَّ لَا يَمُوتُ فِيهَا وَلَا يَحْيَى

'Then he will neither die therein, nor live (a desirable life).' *(87:13)*

Ninety per cent of patients admitted to mental institutes are those embroiled in illicit relationships, whether this is due to online, on-screen, cinema, TV, paper, soft/hard pornographic viewing or reading.

3. *If after ogling, a person becomes involved in sin due to illicit relationship, then both lover and beloved become disgraced forever. They will never truly be able to look each other in the eye. Just as a benevolent father wishes his son to live with nobility and not fall into any misdemeanour, the unlimited Mercy of Allah ﷻ desires His servants not*

to become entangled in any inferior or disgraceful acts. Allah ﷻ *wishes us to live with chivalry, honour, God-Fear (taqwa) and be contented upon permissible (halâl) whilst patiently refraining from impermissible (harâm). Whilst worldly people pacify their vision with temporary, extremely limited and precarious worldly pleasures, Allah* ﷻ *wishes His faithful servants to pacify their vision with the everlasting pleasure of His worship and remembrance:*

Upon the malevolent gazer falls the curse of Rasoolullah ﷺ:

لعن الله الناظر و المنظور اليه

'The curse of Allah is upon the malevolent gazer and the person who invites towards gazing (i.e. the person who parades immodestly).' (Mishkaat)

Those who fear the curse of pious people should tremble at this warning of Rasoolullah ﷺ. May Allah ﷻ protect all of us. The charm of beauty is but for a few days; after a short time body contours changes and in old age all features weather:

'Whilst here geography changes, over there time knows no domain;

neither does her history linger, nor do my chronicles remain.'

Allah ﷻ reveals:

إِنَّ اللهَ خَبِيْرٌ بِمَا يَصْنَعُوْنَ

'And Allah is Aware of all.'

Why has Allah ﷻ attributed the deed of evil gazing to an art (*san'at*)? What is the wisdom behind this analogy? In reality, the person who gazes, pines away his time by drawing-up and desiring his beloved's features in his heart. In his mind, he will caress, cuddle and kiss her, etc., etc. This is why Allah ﷻ is warning of His Awareness of such surreptitious thoughts...

'Tell the believing men that they must lower their gazes and guard their private parts; it is more decent for them. Surely Allah is All-Aware of what they do.' (Glorious Qur'ān, 24:30)

'Allamah Aloosee Baghdadi ﷺ highlights four features of this Verse in his commentary *Roohul Ma'ani*:

1.　Allah ﷻ is fully Aware of the ever roaming nature of your gaze.

2.　Allah ﷻ is fully Aware of how the malevolent gazer employs all of his four faculties: his vision (*basirah*); his ears (*sim'aah*); his taste (*zaiqah*) and smell (*shamah*) to acquire perverted pleasures.

3.　Allah ﷻ is also fully Aware of the bodily movements that a malevolent gazer employs to acquire his beloved; the actions of his hands, feet, etc., etc.

4.　Allah ﷻ is also fully Aware of the ultimate aim and purpose of the malevolent gazer. In this final warning, a hidden threat is concealed. A dreadful beating and punishment awaits.

In my time as a medical practitioner I have met numerous patients submerged in this illness of malevolent gazing and affairs. All complain of the same symptoms: restlessness, constriction, depression, sleeplessness, turmoil, living hell, suicidal thoughts, ill health, palpating heart, weak mind, lack of enthusiasm or interest in any activity. I always reply, 'This is the punishment for evil gazing/unlawful relationship and what happens when you give your heart to anybody besides Allah ﷻ.' That beauty who struts upon earth today will be a pile of dust tomorrow. Open her grave after she dies and all you will observe will be mud. If you were to ask, 'Which part of you were the rosé cheeks? The perfectly shaped fair nose? The brunette hair? The green eyes?'

Soil is all you will observe. For trial and examination purposes, Allah ﷻ

has embellished this earth with distemper (an art technique used to render theatrical scenery) to observe who perishes upon such murals and who succeeds by following the Prophetic teachings? If such dazzling beauties and models were not to stroll upon this earth, what kind of examination and test would it be? Therefore do not be deceived by these frescos for many a seeker of Deen have been deluded in this way and failed to reach Allah ﷻ. Even before death, as old age appears the object of love and admiration withers from grace and beauty. The lover now unreservedly rushes and returns from the cemetery having buried his beloved of yesteryear:

'Which rosy cheek am I enshrouding? The coffin of my beauty I am burying,

endearing such perishable models is futile O men of understanding.'

In the final analysis, only Allah ﷻ is worthy of true love, because His ﷻ beauty and splendour are not only everlasting; every moment He ﷻ increases in Grandeur...

'...Everyday He is in a state of accomplishment.' (Glorious Qur'ān, 55:29)

Reduction or annihilation of an attribute of Allah ﷻ is impossible. In complete contrast, at every moment, the attractiveness of worldly beauties is in decline. Sooner or later their bodies will be lowered into graves; the silky black hair will grey; the back and bosom will haunch and sag; eyes will drip with water and faces will wilt. Upon what are you wasting your life? When you keep this ultimate ending of all beauties in front of you, then striving and refraining from gazing becomes easy. However, you should understand this thought process is merely a ploy to dupe one's self (*nafs*), for in reality it is the lowest form of servitude (to Allah ﷻ), because it implies; if these beauties were not to perish we would have been fixated by them. The highest form of submission (*abdiyat*) is to acknowledge and inculcate such affection, respect and gratitude for the Being and Favours of Allah ﷻ that even if the beauty of such models were not to perish until Qiyamah and beyond, we would still not raise an eyelid to look at them out of awe and veneration for the Command of Allah ﷻ. Whatever joy and happiness is acquired at expense of the Displeasure of Allah ﷻ is in reality no delight but an accursed bargain.

Moreover, any fickle pleasure acquired from sin hides umpteen unpleasantness's and sorrows. Merely scheming about sinning is a sign of distance from Allah ﷻ and a means of acquiring His Punishment. What possibility of inner tranquillity or peace when a virus has entered the heart and made it a carcass. Notwithstanding its current life form this beauty will one day be a corpse, accordingly whenever it enters the heart it brings along its characteristic of annihilation. It is therefore impossible for such a heart to enjoy the closeness and pleasure of Allah ﷻ. Consider an analogy, you are sitting in a resplendent room, eating the most sumptuous of dishes when a coffin is brought in and left there. What happens to your appetite? Similarly, when a corpse enters the heart how may the pleasure of Relationship with Allah ﷻ remain? Allah ﷻ does not enter such an heart wherein are the thoughts, stench and filth of impermissible one's.

This is why the pious (*Ahlullah*), at all times, are conscientious of their heart thereby preventing the self (*nafs*) from bringing any forbidden pleasures into their mind. Moreover, they avoid even the remotest possible viewing of any such images which have been prohibited. No doubt a small amount of sorrow is experienced, however the blessings of this grief is constant alertness, tranquillity and proximity of Allah ﷻ.

When the sun is about to rise, the eastern horizon becomes red...a sign of sunrise. Similarly, whosoever bleeds his heart red in refraining from impermissible desires, then this is a sign of the imminent arrival of Divine Proximity.

In complete contrast those who do not protect their vision, sooner or later ruin themselves by falling into unlawful relationships. The subsequent experience of torment is very real here in this world; many die uttering the name of their beloved instead of the name of Allah ﷻ and the *Kalimah*. This is why the Mashā'ikh describe association with impermissible women and young boys as venomous poisons. When Shaytan becomes despondent upon trying to mislead a devotee, he employs the guile of such women and young boys. These weapons of his are so powerful that whosoever falls prey to them suffers enormous and catastrophic harm; because other sins do not distance one from Allah ﷻ as these two forms of transgression. For example, crimes like lying, backbiting, stealing or failure to pray *salāh* with *jama'at* would disorientate a person's heart from Allah ﷻ by 45 degrees. Nevertheless, if they repent the heart once again aligns itself towards Allah ﷻ. However, when somebody becomes embroiled in an illicit relationship: alignment of their heart is now 180 degrees away from Allah ﷻ; the entire orientation (*qiblah*) of the heart is completely in an opposite direction. Even when such a person prays salāh, recites the Qur'ān, makes *thikr*, at all time the image of his beloved (a soon to be decomposed corpse) and not the thought of Allah ﷻ is in front of him. No greater separation from Allah ﷻ takes place due to sin as happens when one becomes involved in this calamity. When a hunter wishes to catch a bird, he entraps its wings thereby preventing it from flying. Similarly when Shaytan observes a devotee rapidly progressing in the Path of Allah ﷻ, saving himself from all sins, then he tries to ensnare him in some form of illicit love thereby totally depriving him of Allah ﷻ. Accordingly, irrespective of how beautiful the illegal image in front of us, never ever raise your gaze towards her. Despite being able to view, become temporally blind. Will Allah ﷻ not love such a honourable person to whom He has blessed vision? Wherever Allah ﷻ

wishes us to look we observe; whatever He wishes us to refrain from looking at we shun. To please Him, we sacrifice and throttle our desires; in the process we experience grief. Consequently, we become His beloved for Allah ﷻ enters such a broken heart.

Shaykh 'Abdul Ghanee Phulphuri ﵫ used to say, 'Light a fire in front of a ripe fruit laden tree and all of its produce, leafs and branches will be lost. Only after a lot of work; pruning, nursing and irrigation over a period of years is there any hope of the tree returning to its former glory. Similarly, the *nur* which is acquired from *thikr*, obedience, recitation of salāh and Glorious Qur'ān, etc., etc.; frolicking in malevolent gazing just once is enough to cause annihilation of the heart and whatever spirituality was acquired. To regain this wealth and state of the heart through obedience is a long arduous process. The oppression of gazing is difficult to overcome, only after much repentance and constant protection of one's vision does the heart stand any chance of regaining spiritual rejuvenation.

When we say, 'We are unable to save ourselves from sin.' In reality we are admitting to our lack of courage, for if forgoing sins was impossible Allah ﷻ would not have revealed...

$$وَذَرُوا۟ ظَاهِرَ ٱلْإِثْمِ وَبَاطِنَهُ$$

'Leave aside all sins, externally (zaahire) and esoteric (baatine)...' (6:120)

This Command is sufficient proof that we have the capacity to forgo all sins, because Allah ﷻ would never Command any concept beyond our control...

$$لَا يُكَلِّفُ ٱللَّهُ نَفْسًا إِلَّا وُسْعَهَا$$

'There is no imposition on the self beyond its ability...' (2:286)

In reality we always act in accordance with the favour and whim of our self (nafs), this is why we are submerged in sin. Whereas our self is, in reality, our biggest enemy, whose enmity we have been forewarned about by Rasoolullah ﷺ...

إِنَّ أَعدَاع عدوّک فی جنبیک

'Your biggest enemy is within you.'

If a sworn antagonist were to present you with a box of chocolates, would you accept or be suspicious of his intentions? Are they laced with poison? Regrettably, despite knowing of the enmity of our *nafs*, we pamper to its every suggestion to view a forbidden object. Ostentatiously, it appears a call towards pleasure, in reality it is a pathway to punishment. Besides the harms of the Hereafter, in this world the heart becomes agitated; sleep will disappear and one becomes distanced from Allah ﷻ. Malevolent gazing is a sin of absolute stupidity. You will not gain her, therefore why traumatise your heart? Is it not foolish to stare at another's belongings? Is anything ever acquired by lustful glancing? Even if she were to become yours, there is no tranquillity because there is nothing besides sorrow, grief and sadness in any entity which results in the Displeasure of Allah ﷻ. He is the Creator of joy and unhappiness. Whosoever undergoes grief to save himself from sins and to Please Allah ﷻ, then Allah ﷻ causes such a heart to experience tranquillity even without the means of happiness. Waves of joy overcome such a person, such ecstasy which even kings are not able to enjoy. Whosoever displeases Allah ﷻ then He ﷻ makes such a person's existence bitter...

وَمَنْ أَعْرَضَ عَنْ ذِكْرِيْ فَإِنَّ لَهُ مَعِيْشَةً ضَنْكًا

'Whosoever refrains from My remembrance, I will embitter his life.'

Whosoever is submerged in this sin and wishes to be extradited from it should adopt these six avenues:

1. Make use of the courage which Allah ﷻ has endowed you.

2. Make du'a for resolution from Allah ﷻ.

3. Request the pious, especially one's Deeni benefactor (e.g. Shaykh or Ustadh) to make du'a for courage.

4. Be constant with the Remembrance (*thikr*) of Allah ﷻ.

5. Stay far and detached from viewing impermissible beauties.

6. Regularly sit in the company of the pious and establish a relationship and bond with them.

Never become despondent on the propensity of love, for this power in itself is a valuable commodity, it is a question of application. Whichever aeroplane has a powerful engine and is served by a full tank of fuel will rapidly reach its destination as long it travels in the right direction. However, if it is misdirected away from the Ka'bah, it will just as rapidly travel in the wrong and opposite direction. The power of love is a form of energy; if through the company of a pious person and remembrance of Allah ﷻ it is correctly employed, then such a person very rapidly traverses the Path of Allah ﷻ in such a short period of time; which a person deprived of love would have taken years to travel. Accordingly, some fornicators, when they have inclined towards Allah ﷻ, have reached Him through one sigh of regret and repentance. Under the supervision of some Shaykh, their progress was just as prolific as their decline...from grovelling in dens to heights of heavenly elevation...

'Used to associate with impermissible beauties did I,

now keep the company of pious do I.

Never hold in contempt the sinful o my,

for they could enjoin themselves to Allah ﷻ with one sigh.'

ഇൗരു

Prescription For Malevolent Gazing & Illicit Relationships

*S*haykh Hakeem Muhammad Akhtar *hafizahullah* continues, 'In Light of the Glorious Qur'ān, Hadeeth and statements of the pious I relate a comprehensive prescription which will, *inshā'Allah,* prove to be a cure for even the most severe form of malevolent gazing and illicit relationship; no matter how entrenched the habit. Within a short while of adopting this remedy, *inshā'Allah,* you will feel as if your are walking upon the Plain of Hereafter; vividly perceiving Paradise (*Jannah*) and Hell (*Jahannam*); whilst the impermissible desires and pleasures of this world will appear inferior.

1.   Prayer of Repentance (*Salat-ut-Taubah*)

Appoint a time in solitude, wear clean clothes, apply perfume (*it'r*) and pray two rakats *Salat-ut-Taubah*. Thereafter, seek forgiveness from Allah ﷻ for all sins committed,

> *'O Allah ﷻ! From when I have reached maturity, whatever and all sins my eyes have committed; my heart, mind and body have plotted and experienced impermissible pleasures, O Allah ﷻ I repent and seek forgiveness. I promise never to commit any sin and thereby displease you. O Allah ﷻ! Although my sins are endless, nevertheless Your Mercy (Rahmat) is infinitely greater than my sins; therefore through the blessings of Your Munificence forgive all my sins. O Allah ﷻ! You are the Most Forgiving and love to Forgive, therefore forgive and overlook all my sins.'*

2.   Prayer of Need (*Salat-ul-Hajah*)

Thereafter pray two rakats *Salat-ul-Hajah* and make du'a, 'O Allah ﷻ! Have mercy upon my wasted sinful life and reform me. Extricate and free me from the bondage of my *nafs* and grant me the honour of worshipping and obeying You. Grant me enough of Your fear which saves me from Your disobedience. O Allah ﷻ! I ask of You only You.'

'Some ask of You what and some ask You for what, O Creator! I seek You Divine.

When You become mine, the heavens are mine, the earth is mine,

And if You are not mine, then nothing is mine!'

3.   Dhikr of Negation & Confirmation (*Nafee & Isbāt*)

Thereafter recite *La'illaha Illallah* (There is no God but Allah ﷻ) 300 times with the thought, 'With La'illaha purify the heart of everyone besides Allah ﷻ and with *Illallah* the love of Allah ﷻ is entering the heart.

4.   Dhikr of Allah ﷻ (*Ism Zāt*)

At some time recite the name of Allah ﷻ three hundred times. When the word Allah ﷻ emerges from the tongue imagine the word is also coming from your heart with extreme love and affection in the way you would recall your parents when far away from them. If this amount of reverence in the heart is not perceived then at least imitate the People of Divine Love (*Ahl-e-Muhabbat*). This name of Allah ﷻ is extremely valuable, when it appears upon the tongue it always benefits and enlightens.

5.   Special Dhikr of Allah (*Ism Zāt*)

Thereafter recite the name of Allah ﷻ one hundred times with the thought the voice is emerging from every hair and sinew of my body. After a few days extend the thought to include the heavens, stars, planets, skies, seas, land and mountains...that the Glorious Name of Allah ﷻ is emerging from all of Creation.

6. Contemplation Upon Verse: 'Does he not know Allah is Watching?' (Glorious Qur'an, 96:14)

Thereafter contemplate (*muraqabah*) upon the Vision and All-Encompassing Knowledge of Allah ﷻ. For a few minutes ponder, 'Allah ﷻ is watching me and I am sitting in front of my True Benefactor and praying, 'O Allah ﷻ! Ground this reality in my heart that You are watching me whereby I am unable to sin because when this concept and thought is ever present I will not have the courage to disobey.'

Learn to communicate with Allah ﷻ in your heart, 'O Allah ﷻ! When I was malevolently gazing, your Perfect Power and Wrath was observing me, You could have submerged in some illness, calamity or instructed the earth to swallow this wretched one whereby all of creation would have become aware of my misdemeanour. O Allah ﷻ! It was only through Your Tolerance and Favour that You did not reprimand me otherwise I would have been destroyed.'

7. Contemplation Upon Death & Grave

Thereafter reflect upon your death for a few moments. All your beloved, wife, children, relatives, friends and well-wishers all will bid farewell to you. Your clothes will be removed off your body with scissors, you will be bathed, shrouded and taken out of your house forcefully and lowered into a pit. Nobody will stay or aid you now. Only your good deeds will be of any use... '*The grave is either an orchard from the gardens of Paradise or a pit from the hollows of Hell.*' (Hadeeth)

The four senses through which pleasures were experienced are now dormant. The eyes which feasted upon impermissible beauties are now blind. The ears which listened to music are now deaf, the tongue which tasted a thousand delights is now dumb. Only good deeds, acts of worship and taqwa will benefit now. Planks are being placed and soil is being thrown upon you.

Excessive remembrance of death turns the heart away from worldly preoccupations and becomes a means for acquiring ability (tawfeeq) to practise good:

> *'Remember in abundance death, the shatterer of all delights.'*

> *(Bukhāri)*

Reflect upon death so frequently that dread for it is replaced by longing: for in reality, for a Believer (*Mu'min*), death is an invitation from the True Beloved for a meeting. After death is eternal bliss and comfort.

8.   Contemplation Upon Resurrection (Hashr)

Thereafter, contemplate a few minutes upon resurrection on the Plain of Hashr, standing for accounting before Allah ﷻ Who is addressing...

> *'O shameless one! Were you not ashamed to forgo Us and gawk upon a corpse? Was this Our due? Is this why We created you to become infatuated upon another and not remember Us? Did We grant you vision for this purpose? O shameless one! Did we bestow all these bounties: eyes, ears and heart in order to employ them in Our disobedience? There will then follow a series of Commands for the sinful ones:*

$$\text{خُذُوْهُ فَغُلُّوْهُ. ثُمَّ الْجَحِيْمَ صَلُّوْهُ.}$$

> *'Apprehend them! Enchain them! Cast them into Hell!'* (6:30-31)

Thereafter, crying profusely seek forgiveness from Allah ﷻ and protection from His anger; supplicate (du'a) for reformation of one's behaviour and death with faith (imaan).

9. Contemplation Upon Punishment of Hell

Thereafter contemplate upon Hell, in such a way as if it is in front of you and you are talking to Allah ﷻ, 'O Allah ﷻ! This is the Fire which You have alighted; People of Hell will be encased within massive columns of fire the pain of which will reach unto the soul. When their skins are scorched to embers You will replenish their skin to suffer punishment all over again. When they become hungry, they will be forced-fed thorns and prickles. When they become thirsty, they will be forced to drink boiling water in the manner in which a thirsty camel drinks (around 125 litres in one sitting and they drink up to 25 litres per minute), as a result their intestines will disintegrate and emerge from their anus. They will wander between Fire and boiling water; attempts to escape will be futile as they are pushed back into Hell to cry tears of blood, They will plead for Your Clemency wherein You will declare, 'Remain disgraced in Hell therein and do not address Me.' O Allah ﷻ! When we are unable to tolerate even a spark of this world how will we endure the Fire of Hell which is seventy times more intense? O Allah ﷻ! Although I am worthy of Hell, I beseech Your Mercy to decree for us salvation from the torment of Hell.'

Repeat this final plea three times with tears, if you are unable to cry then make the appearance of a heartbroken one. Be constant with this method and slowly but surely your *Imaan* will increase until a day arrives when you vividly begin to perceive Hell and your nerve to disobey and sin is broken insha'Allah.

10.　Contemplation Upon Gifts From Allah ﷻ

Thereafter reflect upon the favours and gifts of our Creator and beseech Allah ﷻ in such a way: 'O Allah ﷻ! My soul had not requested an existence; You had granted this Bounty and Favour without asking. Neither had my soul requested an existence in human form; it is Your Favour and Bounty You created me as a human (*Ashraful Makhluq*) and not in the shape of a dog or pig. Moreover, had you allowed me to be born in a non-Muslim home I would have been in immortal danger and harm even if it had been in a royal or wealthy household. You, through Your Favour's have created and endowed without questioning, birth in a Muslim home and gifted nobility as a consequence. You have blessed us with the bounty of Imaan, a gift more precious than everything else in the Universe, again without any asking from us. O Allah ﷻ! When these are Your Bounties and Favours awarded without asking, how is it possible for You to deprive someone when he does ask? O Allah ﷻ! Through the blessings of Your unrequested Bounties and Favours I beseech reformation of my self (*tazkiyah nafs*) in order to be saved from Your disobedience until my last breath.

O Allah ﷻ! Having granted me birth in a Muslim home You blessed me with companionship of Your pious servants and ability to practise upon Deen; for many are those born in Muslim homes but deprived of practising good and some are off-track trapped in association with misguided ones. O Allah ﷻ! You have granted the company of Sulahaa in this world, through Your Favours also grant their company in the Hereafter. O Allah ﷻ! How many sins have I committed; which Your Might and Dominance observed; however Your Forbearance and Forgiveness overlooked and hid them from general knowledge saving me disgrace. O Allah ﷻ! May my thousand lives be sacrificed upon this Leniency, for even if today You were to reveal my shortcomings to humanity all those around me would flee and not allow me to sit or associate with them. O Allah ﷻ! Through Your Grace destine and grant my death upon Imaan. O Allah ﷻ! Through Your Favours appoint immediate entry into Paradise for me.'

Reflect upon each and every bounty of Allah ﷻ; the health, life, wealth, respect, ease, etc., etc., which He has granted and express your gratitude.

Finally, 'O Allah ﷻ! Your Favours and Gifts are incalculable, infinite and beyond reckoning, however whatever little I have been able to contemplate and those which I am unable to comprehend I attempt to express my gratitude with my lips and each and every atom of my body; O Allah ﷻ! Through Your Mercy grant me *tazkiyah nafs*.'

11. Concern For Protection of Gaze

Those who travel to town and city centres for work, offices, study and shopping should pray two rakaats *Salāt-ul-Hājah* and beseech, 'O Allah ﷻ! I place my vision and heart in Your Protection for Thou are the best of Protectors.' Stay in the state of ablution (*wudhu*) as far as possible and occupy your tongue in *dhikrullah*. Even after such precaution, should any shortcomings occur, then make repentance upon every error by performing four rakāts nafl salāh; donate some money in charity (*sadaqah*) according to your means. Be grateful (*shukr*) for all those occasions when you are saved from lustful gazing.

12. Contemplation Upon Ending of Beauty

Whenever your gaze falls upon a beauty, immediately divert your attention away by either contemplating or looking at an ugly object. Reflect upon an extremely old, dark-skinned, scruffy dressed, flat nosed, protruding teeth, blind, bold, obese, lame, coughing, runny nose and smelly person with flies surrounding her. Reflect how this will be the condition of the beauty you have just viewed; when she dies, her skin and body will bloat and rot with a smell which will be unbearable. What benefit is there in becoming captivated by such a perishable entity? However, such reflection will work for a while only. Your self (nafs) will urge to look at her again, this is the real trial, adopt courage, remember Allah in abundance, reflect upon His Punishment and transfix this in your heart. Adopt the company of a pious scholar, somebody who is appointed by a Shaykh.

13.   Most Effective Prescription For Tazkiyah Nafs

The most effective prescription for reformation of the self (*tazkiyah nafs*) is to adopt the company of a pious scholar with regularity and to benefit from his enthusiasm and love for Allah ﷻ because without companionship of the *Ahlullah*, reformation (*islaah nafs*) and firmness (*istiqaamat*) upon Deen is near impossible. Establish a spiritual relationship with whichever pious Shaykh (*Ahlullah*) you feel you have a rapport; regularly inform him of your condition (via letter, email or phone) and practise upon whatever methodology he prescribes with full confidence. *Insha'Allah*, in this way very quickly you will attain recovery from all spiritual ailments. Remain firm upon his teachings and only follow his instructions as regards to form and quantity of *dhikr*.

14.   Contemplation Upon Harms of Lustful Gazing

Regularly reflect upon the harms of lustful gazing; a poisonous and fatal illness; with many who subsequently become submerged in illicit relationships plagued until their last breath; and instead of reciting the *Kalimah* they die babbling nonsense in a state of disbelieve (*kufr*).

haykh Abrar-ul-Haqq Hardoi ﷺ advises,

a)   Whenever ladies *(masturaat)* pass, resolutely lower your gaze no matter how strong the self *(nafs)* urges to view.

b)   If you do raise your gaze upon somebody, immediately lower it, no matter how difficult or bitter and even if it appears you will die of anguish.

c)   Constantly remember by not controlling your gaze the danger remains of being disgraced in this world; the ability *(nur)* of worship being snatched with harm in the Hereafter a certitude.

d)   Upon each misdemeanour of lustful gazing perform 12 rakaats nafl salāh, abundance of repentance *(istighfaar)* and *sadaqat* according to means.

e)   Remember through the tyranny of lustful gazing one's heart *(qalb)* becomes oppressed and this darkness only disappears after many, many occasions of controlling your gaze when the urge arises (prevention is better than cure).

f)   Reflect how through ogling, attraction, thereafter affection and then blind love arises. Through such impermissible infatuations both this world and the Hereafter are destroyed.

g)   Through acts of voyeurism, the enthusiasm for obedience and worship is slowly reduced until a state is reached where they become almost impossible to perform and thereafter also unappealing.

15.   Prescription For Illicit Love & Relationships

 $\bigcirc\!\!\!\!\mathcal{S}$ haykh Hakeem Muhammad Akhtar *hafizahullah* continues, 'If any Muslim becomes embroiled in an illicit relationship then they need to also take note of the following:

a)   Totally and completely cut all relationship and contact with the beloved; talking, meeting (regular, occasional or momentary), viewing, texting, writing, emailing, phoning, etc. Even if another person tries to raise their mention in a conversation, then immediately bring the discussion to a close. Adopt such aloofness from the beloved that even a chance meeting or viewing is not possible. Total and absolute separation.

b)   If there is the possibility of your beloved trying to contact or meet you, then initiate such an argument or quarrel (within the law) that there remains no possibility of a future relationship.

c)   Do not deliberately bring thoughts about the beloved nor reflect upon past encounters and meetings to derive pleasure in the heart; as this too is abuse of trust, sinful and destructive for the soul and more harmful than even illicit gazing.

d)   Totally refrain from reading love stories, novels, viewing films, videos, programs, games, Internet videos, viral magazines and those newspapers which display immoral pictures. Also stay away from all those locations where sin and immoral display takes place (wedding halls, shopping centres, public beaches, theme parks, etc, etc) and refrain from associating with sinful people.

e)   Reflect upon the treachery, disloyalty and betrayal of worldly beauties; even after a person spends all his energies, effort and wealth upon them and another appears more appealing to them;

they will jilt their existing lover for another; sometimes even resorting to foul play to be separated from the former.

f) The day your beloved dies, you will, of a surety, hasten to bury them; similarly, when you die your lover will become disenchanted from your body and also hasten to bury you. Also, if the beauty or health of either deteriorates; all fascination, appeal and lust vapourises. It appears in a Hadeeth, 'Love whosoever you wish; you have to separate from them one day.'

g) Act upon these advises with diligence, resolve and determination; *insha'Allah* all illicit longing and craving will gradually weaken; however do not envisage they will totally disappear. The aim is for inordinate desires to become so weak as to allow control with ease. By behaving in this manner, *insha'Allah* a day will arrive when you achieve control over the self (*nafs*) and attain salvation from love of entities declared forbidden by Allah ﷻ; your soul will then at all times experience celestial bounties; such peace and tranquillity which worldly kings and personalities have never dreamt of. The previous living Hell will become a living Paradise.

'O Allah ﷻ! In mujahadah (opposing the self) You ask half an existence;

Yet bestow a thousand lives and gifts which are spiritually quintessence.'

h) Daily perform two rakaats optional (*nafl*) salāh (preferably when going to sleep at night); thereafter with utmost humility and devotion plead for reformation of the self (*tazkiyah nafs*) because without the Favours and Mercy of Allah ﷻ nobody is able to achieve purity of the *nafs*.

Harms of Illicit Viewing

*S*haykh Hakeem Muhammad Akhtar *hafizahullah* narrates:

1. Impious Servant of Allah ﷻ

'Tell the believing men that they must lower their gazes and guard their private parts; it is more decent for them. Surely Allah is All-Aware of what they do.' (Glorious Qur'ān, 24:30)

Whosoever indulges in ogling is transgressing and violating Verses of the Glorious Qur'ān and thereby involved in haram. Accordingly, to be saved from illicit viewing it is sufficient to reflect on this violation of the Glorious Qur'ān and transgression to Allah ﷻ.

2. Abuse of Trust (*Khiyãnah*)

'He knows the treachery of the eyes and whatever is concealed by hearts.' (Glorious Qur'ān, 40:19)

Revelation of the word treachery (*khiyãnah*) testifies to the fact we are not owners of our eyesight, merely trustees; this is why suicide is forbidden (*haram*) because we are not the owners of our bodies. As trustees we are not allowed to self-harm or employ any faculty as we wish and in conflict with the Owner's wishes; accordingly whoever ogles is treacherous and such a person cannot be the friend (*Walee*) of Allah ﷻ:

'The thief of vision cannot attain the crown of Friendship (walee); Whoever does not aspire for piety cannot be termed a Friend (walee).'

3. Title of Accursed (*Mal'oon*)

The illicit voyeur becomes recipient of the curse of Rasoolullah ﷺ, it appears in Mishkaat Shareef,

'Allah ﷻ curses both the viewer and viewed.'

Whosoever ogles as well as the person who displays their beauty, both are cursed. If illicit viewing was a minor misdemeanour then Mercy of Both Worlds, Leader of all Prophets Muhammad ﷺ would not have made such a statement and du'a; for curse refers to distance from the Mercy of Allah ﷻ. Imam Ra'ghib al-Isfahani ﷫ (died 502 AH ~ 1108 CE) defines curse (*la'nat*) in *Al-Mufradat fi Gharib al-Qur'an* as:

$$البعد عن الرحمة$$

Whosoever becomes distanced from the Mercy (*Rahmah*) of Allah ﷻ is unable to save themselves from wickedness of the self (*nafsul ammarah*) because only the person is able to be saved who is under the Shade of Allah's ﷻ Mercy...

> *'And I do not absolve my inner self of blame. Surely, man's inner self often incites to evil, unless my Lord shows Mercy. Certainly, my Lord is Most-Forgiving, Very-Merciful.'*
>
> (Glorious Qur'an, 12:52)

Whosoever protects his vision, through the blessings of compliance with Divine Decree is saved from the curse of Rasoolullah's ﷺ du'a; and thereby enters the Shade of Allah's ﷻ Mercy. Moreover, ones private parts are also protected from sin.

4. Fool (ahmaq) & Unintelligent

Shaykh Ashraf 'Ali Thānwi ﷫ narrates, 'All sins are a sign of folly and lack of intelligence; because the sinner testifies to this in displeasing his Creator, Who is in total control of the servant's life and death, health and illness, comfort and upheaval, good death or evil death. However, lustful gazing is one of the most foolish sins; neither does she become yours nor are you able to meet her; pine away your life for naught.

Ogling at her will not bring either her beauty or her to you; however your heart becomes restless and perplexed in her remembrance and to vex a Muslim is haram. Accordingly, whosoever stares lustfully, they too are a Muslim and they are vexing their heart by this action. Just as it is haram to vex another Muslim, then how could it be possible to torment, frustrate and aggravate one's own heart?

5. Recipient of Wrath & Curse of Allah ﷻ

If a cynic claims that both in viewing a beauty and in refraining there from the heart is pained; with the latter producing the grief of not knowing what she looks like; then understand both types of pain to be poles apart. The pain of viewing is severe whilst the pain of refraining is infinitely lighter. When you have observed her; an image is recorded in your heart: her figure, complexion, nose, cheeks, lips, eyes, hair and teeth are all noted. This illicit observation will create severe inner turmoil and longing in the heart which will persist because the observer becomes the recipient of the Wrath and Curse of Allah ﷻ; consequently not a moment of tranquillity is enjoyed and life becomes restless and sour. In complete contrast, the pain felt in not viewing her; the missed opportunity is lighter and of short duration; moreover the sweetness of Imaan and Proximity to Allah ﷻ which will be awarded to the heart as a reward for refraining will eclipse all pleasures of this world. The differences in both types of pain are as diverse as the earth and sky; one is the abode of Mercy (*Rahmah*) whilst other is the abode of turmoil. The Command to protect our gaze is a great favour from Allah ﷻ upon the believers; by inflicting us with the lighter regret of not viewing and saving us from the greater turmoil of peeping. This is understood by the similitude of having the choice of either being annoyed by a fly or being bitten by a venomous snake. By not viewing, the pain is synonymous to the pestering of a fly; whilst ogling is more poisonous than a snake bite.

6.   Heart, Organs & Faculties Weakens

'...Undoubtedly, the ears, eyes and heart, of each of them one shall be interrogated.' (17:36)

A voyeur is repeatedly plagued by thoughts of his object of beauty; his heart is constantly pulled hither-thither which affects its vigour and health. All four faculties as well as organs of the body become agitated and incline towards haram. The eyes focus at his object of desire; his ears aim to hear her voice; his tongue wishes to kiss and savour her; his nose wishes to smell her fragrance; his hands wish to caress; his feet desire to walk towards her whilst all along...*'Innallah Khabeerun bema yasna'oon.'* 'Allamah Aloosee 🔮 narrates upon this Verse in *Roohul Ma'ānee...*

بِاجَالَةِ النَّظَرِ بِاسْتِعْمَالِ سَائِرِ الْحَوَاسِّ

'Allah is aware of the voyeur's repeated surreptitious glancing at beauties.'

The purpose behind this warning is to threaten punishment if one does not withhold and repent. Illicit viewing is the first step to adultery with the final stage where private parts become exposed and a person is disgraced in both worlds. This is why the first step has been prohibited; because unchecked it automatically leads unto spiritual destruction. The heart deteriorates and becomes so distanced from Allah 🕌 with apathy and indifference towards good deeds setting in. When physical organs are aroused in a haram manner, it is inevitable physical and spiritual harm must follow: weakening of eyesight; mental and emotional weaknesses; angina; sexual impotency; prostrate problems; masturbation; sexually transmitted diseases; emotional guilt, fear and anxiety; depression, loss of self-esteem and deterioration of health. Moreover infidelity leads unto divorce with successive generations of children suffering. May Allah grant all of us correct Tawfeeq.

$\mathcal{CS}$haykh Mufti Muhammad Shafee' ﷺ narrates, 'The essence of the entire teachings and writings of Shaykh Ashraf 'Ali Thānwi ﷺ may be summarised by his answer to a remedy requested for lustful gazing,

'Aside from courage and endurance there is no other cure. Until you make courage nothing will avail. Enact what is within your control and strength; thereafter plead for the assistance and aid of Allah ﷻ.

Whosoever does not try then how will the Aid of Allah ﷻ arrive?

A chance glance is natural and the Glorious Qur'an has shown a remedy; to keep your gaze lowered and not frequent those venues where the gaze will fall upon non-Mahram (e.g. Wedding Shows, Funeral Parlours, Theme Parks, Shopping Malls, Pleasure Beaches, etc.).

Despite such caution, whenever the gaze does fall, then do not view a second time no matter how strong the urge is from one's own self.

Disciplining and correcting one's self (nafs) in this manner will be rewarded with a great bounty; the heart will be filled with light (nur) of Imaan (faith).'

(Majalis Mufti Azam)

Chapter Nine

The Poisonous Effects

of Immoral Gazing

by

$\mathcal{S}$haykh-ul-Hadeeth

Mawlana Muhammad Saleem Dhorat
hafizahullah

Reviewed

by

Mawlana Maseehullah Patel &

Mawlana Qãri Muhammad 'Abdullah

Rasoolullah ﷺ narrated,

'The gaze is amongst the arrows of Shaytan.'

(Targheeb wat Tarheeb)

Amongst the numerous bounties bestowed by Allah ﷻ one is the favour of eyesight and the sustenance of the eye is vision. Every organ has a mode of provision, for example the stomach's nourishment is liquid and solid edibles. The victuals of the hands is to hold; that of the ears to listen and of the eye to view.

The sustenance of the stomach affects the entire body; deprive it of its nourishment and the repercussions are felt throughout the body. Similarly all organs; eyes, tongue, ears, etc., all need their provisions. If any are deprived of either their sustenance or correct function, then their operation is affected. For example, if somebody were to keep their eyes shut for one month or the hands were to be folded tight for one year, then these organs will be affected for they are being deprived of normal healthy usage.

All these organs are tremendous bounties of Allah ﷻ. We never reflect on these gifts and therefore are always ungrateful, unmindful and envious of what we perceive others to own, 'I am the only one who has been deprived and am not a rich man!' O servants of Allah ﷻ! Place a value to your eyes, ears, tongue, kidneys, liver, heart, brain and other faculties. No sane person would ever exchange any of these faculties for all the wealth of this world.

Similarly, if a pauper was offered a kingdom or even half the world in return for just one eye, then no intelligent person would be willing to do so; he is contented with his bread and lentils. One meagre meal a day is sufficient. Accordingly, this vision, this eyesight is a gift from Allah ﷻ and they too have sustenance; to view. At all times they wish to view hither thither, this and that object, just like the stomach desires to eat various edibles. However, certain foodstuffs are permissible (*halāl*) whilst others are forbidden (*harām*) and it is the Favour and Mercy of Allah ﷻ that over 90% of foodstuff is *halāl* and less than 10% are *harām*.

Permissible & Impermissible

Just as these edibles and nourishment of the stomach have been categorised into *halāl* and *harām* so too are the provisions of all other organs. The faculty of touch is also governed by *halāl* and *harām*; it is permissible to touch such-and-such but forbidden to lay a hand on so-and-so. Similarly, the provision of the tongue is speaking, but this too is divided into two categories; to speak such-and-such words is permissible whilst to relate other forms of language and topics is forbidden. The faculty of hearing is likewise separated, to listen to so-and-so words and sounds are *halāl* whilst listening to other categories is *harām*.

The vision of the eyes too is divided into two categories; to view certain elements is *halāl* whilst the viewing of others is *harām*. It is Allah ﷻ who has created and sent us into this world and decreed ordinances for this body of ours. For each faculty of ours He has decreed the limits of *halāl* and *harām*, this is the trial of our worldly existence. Allah ﷻ wishes to know whether His servant, 5 to 6 foot in length, refrains from listening to backbiting (*gheebah*), vulgar conversations and music? Does My servant restrain himself from lying, false accusations, backbiting, hurling abuse and hurting the feeling of others?

Alhamdulillah, many of us, especially those who are regarded as average practising Muslims are very particular about matters of diet. Edibles of the stomach are categorised, for example to drink water is permissible but to drink alcohol is impermissible; the eating of *halāl* mutton is permissible but to eat pork is impermissible. We scrutinise ingredients when purchasing foodstuff, we even save ourselves from doubtful foods (*mushtabih*) and those outlets which are infamous for unwholesomeness. However, the *taqwa* of this deeni conscious Muslim, who is considered the repository of good deeds, is limited to edibles of the stomach. When it comes to provisions of the other organs, they all become unrestrained: the ears, tongue, eyes, heart and mind all become liberated. The mind and heart instead of thinking positively with *taqwa* and of good are allowed uninhibited freedom.

Whomsoever Strives Acquires

This is my plea in this discourse, to myself firstly and then to all those present, that henceforth we allow all our faculties only permissible sustenance and we save ourselves in all avenues of life from the impermissible. Make a firm and resolute intention, pray to Allah ﷻ and thereafter endeavour...

'Whomsoever strives acquires.'

Whosoever creates a concern to differentiate between *halāl* and *harām* in all activities; between what Pleases and Displeases Allah ﷻ; between correct and incorrect usages of the priceless bounties which Allah ﷻ has endowed us, only such a person is truly successful. If Allah ﷻ had not endowed us these eyes then no physician on earth would be able to grant us vision; if Allah ﷻ had not bestowed these ears, no team of medical experts would be able to grant us hearing; if Allah ﷻ had not bestowed this tongue, nobody would be able to grant us the ability to speak. Nevertheless, how do we repay such priceless gifts and items? By contradicting His Commands and incurring His Displeasure. What ingratitude, what rebellion, what mutiny, how uncouth? Even with a fellow human who may confer a small favour, a single meal or a small loan we do not stoop to such low; we even tolerate and swallow such a person's inordinate and bitter remark despite possessing the ability to extract revenge because we feel indebted to him. This is our behaviour towards the conferrer of small worldly favours; contrast this with our traitorous relationship and rebellion (*ihsaan faramosh*) towards the Creator who showers us with priceless bounties and the *nemat* of *Imaan* from morning till evening.

Make a pledge and firm intention to protect our vision. If you desire spiritual progress, control your eyes, because the Messenger ﷺ of Allah ﷻ has elaborated and described severe repercussions and harms of sinning with this organ. When a person sins with his ears, for example if he were to listen to music, then others would get to know of it. This in itself acts as a barrier and source of shame. When a person swears or indulges in backbiting others become aware. The same is true of all external organs except the eyes, because its surreptitious movements are not visible to others.

Accordingly, even for the most civilised and cultured person, there is nothing besides *taqwa*, besides fear, besides shame, besides humility for Allah ﷻ, no other barrier or power which may constrain and save him from immoral gazing. This is why Shaytan uses and exploits this weakness; notwithstanding the number of Hajj and Umrah, beard, old-age, grey hair and piety which other's observe. Obviously, such a person may not wantonly flout other commands and indulge in music, backbiting, etc., etc, however the self (*nafs*) satiates its craving for sins and rebellion by indulging in immoral gazing without the knowledge of other's.

Arrows of Shaytan

Rasoolullah 襐 narrated,

> *'The gaze is amongst the arrows of Shaytan.'*

(Targheeb wat Tarheeb)

When Shaytan wishes to ensnare a pious person, a deeni conscious person, a seeker of truth, a seeker of self-reformation, a person who forsakes the world, a person who externally appears depressed and forlorn (when in reality he is engrossed in the acquisition of the Pleasure of Allah 襐 and only finds solace in His Remembrance, good deeds, pure environment of the Masjid, company of pious and recitation of the Glorious Qur'an), then Shaytan entraps such a person in immoral gazing. This is the extremely poisonous and venomous arrow of Shaytan which entangles the pious...

> *'Fornication of the eyes is to look.'*

Fornication of the eyes is to view a non-mahram; this is the first step of fornication. Allah 襐 protect all of us for whosoever becomes embroiled in adultery, then the first step would have been committed by the eyes and what appeals to it; thereafter the next step would be verbal communication which Rasoolullah 襐 has described as fornication of the tongue; thereafter the adulterer wishes to gain physical proximity to the adulteress; this is fornication of the hand; now the thoughts of each constantly plague the other; each run towards the other; this is fornication of the feet. This viewing, listening, desiring, touching, fantasising... *'The heart desires.'*

'When am I able to fulfil my craving?' Every time such a person observes or comes into proximity with his beloved, his heart wishes to fulfil his desires. He may pretentiously talk about this-that-and-the-other or present numerous pretexts to converse or meet with her, but this desire remains paramount at all times. The other party may not even be aware, in modern society he or she may be described as only a friend, associate or work colleague, but in reality he or she is the object of carnal desire. This is why the Sharee'ah has forbidden any relationship or contact (verbal, physical or otherwise) with a non-mahram without a valid Sharee' reason.

Privacy With Non-Mahram

Rasoolullah ﷺ narrated,

> *'A man does not meet privately with a woman without Shaytan being the third (present).'* (Muslim)

Our pious have stated, 'Even if a pious man of the calibre of Hasan al-Basri and a pious lady of the rank of Raabia al-Basri were to be together in private, then Shaytan would surely be able to weave his ploy.' The *taqwa* of both would be left on one side and the prophesy of Rasoolullah ﷺ would materialise. These deceiving claims we conjure, 'my heart is pure and devoid of feelings and desire when I speak to non-mahram,' is all nonsense; you may deceive your friends but who is able to deceive Allah ﷻ? If you are devoid of feelings when conversing with non-mahram then why do you ogle at her or him? Why would any Muslim displease his Creator without achieving any form of pleasure? Why would a Muslim undergo such a sacrifice? Incurring the wrath of Allah ﷻ without achieving any transitory joy; is this conceivable or rational?

Accordingly, immoral gazing is the first step towards adultery and illicit viewing encompasses all forms of ogling: in the street, at work, at places of study, shopping, pictures in print, on TV and of course on the Internet. Websites on the latter have obviously exceeded all bounds of decency and morality; even those who have some resemblance of Deen view such despicable images in the privacy of their rooms. Pornography is now rampant on the Internet with lewd images easily accessible; nobody is viewing you except your Creator. Each deed and viewing of yours is being recorded, for which you will have to answer on the Day of Judgement:

'On a day when all the secrets will be searched out. And he will have neither strength (to defend), nor a supporter.'

(Glorious Qur'an, 86:9,10)

Your 'purity' (*taqaddus*) will be rent asunder and exposed; your ogling at women on the streets, on TV, on the Internet will all be revealed. When you watch films, documentaries and even news in the name of enlightenment, what is the state of your heart when you observe attractive presenters for two hours at a time? When this illness increases and takes strength; a state is reached when so many thousands of pictures are now recorded and stored on your hard heart and mind: that even when sitting in the first row (*saff*) in the Masjid in *salāh* and during *du'a* the pictures are flashing in front of you. To all it appears this pious person is engrossed in deep contemplation, whereas he is in another realm; a cyber world. Every image is processed by the eyes and recorded by the heart. O brethren! If you do not repent from this folly with a true heart, then remember, at the time of death when the Angel of Death arrives to extract your soul, this habit of lewd viewing and these bawdy images will come to the fore.

Such a person stoops to such a low that even whilst engaging in conjugal acts with his wife (*halāl*), his heart is elsewhere and fantasising other women (*harām*). O brethren, all this the repercussions of illicit viewing! If you were to repent with a true heart, I take oath that within a few months of sincere striving, all the images in your heart would be wiped away and there will be no perplexity for you in this world, at the time of death or in the Hereafter. Why do we observe such images? For pleasure, pleasure and nothing but pleasure.

Sweetness of Imaan

If a child, fond of chocolates, falls ill and there is fear of his illness increasing if he were to eat chocolates, then parents will present an alternative sweet item, say a piece of fruit. To the child, the strawberry or cherry may not be as appealing, but as soon as he eats it his mind is diverted away from the chocolate. Rasoolullah ﷺ narrated:

'The glance is a poisoned arrow of Shaytan. (Tagheeb wat Tarheeb)

Whoever lowers his gaze for Allah, He will bestow upon him a refreshing sweetness, which he will find in his heart on the day he meets Him.'

When this sweetness of Imaan is experienced then such a person looks forward and is not afraid of lowering his gaze when an impermissible beauty passes by. However, if you fail to address and tackle this illness and it increases in severity, then remember that although your youth may pass and in old-age you lose the virility to commit adultery nevertheless this malady of immoral gazing will increase in strength. In our communities whenever an old-age person visits the household, then teenage girls are encouraged to greet them under the pretext of meeting an old acquaintance of the family. The pious have written, 'Old men are more dangerous than young.' Why? Because, whenever a young person becomes embroiled in illicit viewing he has the strength to dissipate his desires with his wife; in complete contrast when an old man ogles at impermissible women, on account of his lack of virility, he is unable to soothe his desires and they increase in strength. When he places his hand upon a young girl, others assume it is out of paternal affection, not so; this is the hand of desire. When he embraces a young girl, it is not out of paternal care, but out of lustful craving.

This is why purdah applies to both young and old. Purdah is no oppression upon Muslim ladies, it is for their protection, nobody must be able to cast a filthy gaze, strike a filthy hand, give a filthy hug or cast filthy aspersions upon our womenfolk. Islam does not view women as inferior items to be handled by all and sundry as the oriental propaganda machine would have the world believe; rather Islam regards women to be so precious and valuable in rank that no non-mahram may even behold her.

Immoral gazing takes many forms. To view somebody's house, car, properties, possessions, etc., etc., with a covetous view is also impermissible. To ask a sincere and big-hearted friend about an item with avarice knowing full well he will feel compelled to gift it to you is also immoral. To view another's possession with jealousy and envy is also wrong and sinful, 'Why has he got it and not me.'

All these are impermissible use of vision; however the most chronic amongst them is the viewing of non-mahram women. Control and lower your gaze and then notice the tranquillity, peace and serenity in life, *salāh, thikr*, recitation of the Glorious Qur'an. In the beginning, lowering one's gaze appears strenuous. Shaykh Mufti Muhammad Taqee Uthmani *hafizahullah* has described this initial distaste by means of an example. In Saudi Arabia, there is a custom to drink small portions of coffee and *kahwa* (a traditional green tea recipe). When first experienced, *kahwa* appears unappealing, it appears distasteful when drunk the first dozen times or so. However, thereafter one becomes so accustomed and habited to *kahwa* that mere mention of the word or smell pricks the ears and taste buds. Our venerable Shaykh Mufti Taqee *hafizahullah* allegorizes lowering and protecting one's gaze to the initial bitterness of this drink, unappealing, strenuous, difficult and bitter. However, repeated striving and lowering of the gaze transform this exercise into one of pleasure; there is no other way but to repent from displeasing Allah ﷻ.

Those who attend colleges, universities, offices, hospitals, workplaces, etc., (and there are many of my acquaintances who are professionals present here) who are constantly coming into contact with non-mahram women will feel it is impossible to save oneself from illicit viewing. They are probably thinking, 'Yes, we too wish to save ourselves, however you are fortunate to inhabit the four walls of the Masjid and Madrassah whilst we have to daily go into environments wherein free intermingling of the genders take place. What to do?'

Brothers! No Command of Allah ﷻ has been revealed which is impossible to fulfil or practice. If it was then it would imply that when 1400 years ago the Sharee'ah were revealed, Allah ﷻ was unaware that all these Muslim people would come to these shores and be compelled to come into contact with non-mahram; is it conceivable that He could reveal such Verses without knowledge? Could such thoughts ever become the belief of a Muslim? Every Muslim knows that Allah ﷻ is aware of what is to transpire until and beyond Qiyamah; He revealed these Commands with full awareness of circumstances. All we have to do is immediately make a firm intention to keep our gaze lowered. Before leaving the Masjid, pray two *rakaats taubah* and then make a firm pledge and plead with Allah ﷻ to create the means and true understanding even in such environments to save one from this and all sins. First of all acknowledge and accept the harms of this sin; secondly align yourself towards a pious Scholar and authentic Shaykh from the Mashā'ikh and outline this illness of yours and seek his remedy for this malady. Insha'Allah within a short while you will recover. At least make a firm intention and accept the possibility of being cured from this sin.

Internet Viewing

However, certain steps you will have to take. Firstly, regarding the Internet, I offer a theory. Without a genuine reason do not view the Internet, irrespective of whether the thought to view appertains to educational, news, Islam or whatever. Do not view without absolute necessity; ponder upon its name, a web, a trap, whosoever enters it and to whatever extent becomes correspondingly entrapped. I too sometimes need to view the Internet, you come across an interesting article and then another and then another. You too will have experienced this, we view with the intention of spending 10 to 15 minutes but before you realise 1 to 2 hours have passed. If you wish to protect and utilize the valuable seconds of your life, then protect yourself from futility for they are dacoits of time: the robbers of football, cricket, Internet and shisha. Even minimum viewing of the Internet is only for those people who are able to practice self-restrain, as for those who are unable to, then they should not access the Internet at all. You log on to listen to somebody's lecture and end up viewing some film, pornography or other impermissible material. Protect yourself, constantly remember the Verse of the Glorious Quran:

'He knows the treachery of the eyes and whatever is concealed by hearts.' *(Glorious Qur'an, 40:19)*

Secondly, we also have this habit of viewing hither-thither when walking, accordingly whenever a non-mahram woman appears it becomes difficult to control and lower one's gaze. O my brothers! Is it easier to keep one's gaze low from the beginning or when a non-mahram woman appears? Our Sharee'ah teaches us:

'Tell the believing men to lower their gazes...' *(Glorious Qur'an, 24:30)*

'Tell the believing women to lower their gazes...' *(Glorious Qur'an, 24:31)*

What this teaches us is as soon as we leave our homes for the Masjid, shops, workplace or whatever we keep our gaze lowered at all times in the state of *thikr*. We will become oblivious to those on the street; when the need arises to view then look up. Some Commentators have narrated that when Shaytan was expelled from Jannah he vowed 'O Allah ﷻ! Keep me alive until Qiyamah?' 'Very well, you had been destined to stay alive until Qiyamah anyway.'

> *'Then I will come upon them from their front side and from*
> *their behind, and from their right and from their left. You will*
> *not find most of them grateful.'* (*Glorious Qur'an, 7:17*)

Shaytan had vowed to appear from all sides except two; from above and below. One group of Commentators have narrated this descriptive use of language as implying in Arabic that he will appear form all sides. Another group of Commentators aver his claim of appearing from in front, from behind and from left and right implies his attack from above and below is weak. Therefore, we have two choices either to walk looking upwards or downwards to be saved from sinful viewing. However in viewing upwards there is the danger of tripping therefore there is only one realistic way and that is to lower the gaze and thereby reach Allah ﷻ with peace and ease.

Protect your gaze, especially those who are compelled to enter obnoxious environments. Make a pledge, and then at least there will be some reduction from your habitual illicit viewing umpteen times a day. Even if there is a reduction of one daily, through the blessings of repentance *insha'Allah* one day you will become completely cured. Daily, before leaving home for your occupation plead to Allah ﷻ, 'O Allah ﷻ! I have been submerged in this sin for so long, never acknowledging or attempting to become free from it, today I pledge to save myself, O Allah ﷻ protect me.'

Remain alert throughout the day and at night pray, meditate, self-analyse and seek Allah's ﷻ help and an alternative avenue of income and; if this is your predestined occupation then seek the courage, strength and determination to save oneself from violating this Command. Our problem is we just do not try. This is my appeal to those who are enjoined to some Shaykh; those who are traversing the path of moral-reformation must understand that until you do not save yourself from immoral gazing you will not progress spiritually. Why? You make *dhikr*, you adopt the company of pious, you recite the Qur'an; all these good deeds produce spiritual tranquillity and breeze, however you are not protecting your gaze, therefore this tranquil breeze will not be able to soothe and comfort you. Just like in an air-conditioned car or room, if the window is left open the cool air will disappear. The tranquil breeze produced by your acts of worship is escaping through the breach of your eyes. Similarly the warmth of Divine Love produced in your heart by adoration of Allah ﷻ is also escaping through incorrect gazing. This is why, despite years of worship and performance of salāh, the condition of the heart remains stagnant and the quality of deeds as it were. Therefore, quickly close this breach of the eyes and then observe how your heart warms to the Love of Allah ﷻ. May Allah ﷻ grant all of us tawfeeq.

Pearls of Wisdom of Sayyidduna Luqman ﷺ

*S*ayyidduna Luqman ﷺ *stayed in the company of 4,000 Prophets* ﷺ *and the essence of knowledge which he acquired from them he formulated in a number of advises:*

1. *When in Salāh, protect your heart.*

2. *When sitting down to eat, protect your throat.*

3. *When you visit somebody's residence protect your gaze.*

4. *When amongst people, protect your tongue.*

5. *Always remember two things; Allah* ﷻ *and death.*

6. *Always forget two things: forget for ever the favours you enact to anybody. Secondly, whenever somebody acts inappropriately towards you, then forget it. (Ruhul Ma'ani)*

A Heart Rendering Incident of Illicit Viewing

Shaykh-ul-Hadeeth Zakariyya Khandalwi ﷺ

With additional notes from the

Islaahi Mawa'iz

of

Shaykh Mufti Muhammad Yousuf Ludhyaanwi ﷺ

haykh-ul-Hadeeth Zakariyya ✿ narrates, 'There is an amazing incident related by Hakeemul Ummat ✿, his Deputies Shaykh Muhammad 'Easa ✿ in *Anfas 'Easa*, Shaykh Mufti Muhammad Shafee' ✿ and also by my father Shaykh Yahya Khandhalvi ✿...There are numerous lessons for all of us in this episode, (the two most important being not to consider or view anybody with contempt and secondly the degree of faith and affection one should harbour for one's Shaykh...even if, Allah ✿ Forbid, he becomes embroiled in a monumental calamity).

This incident took place towards the end of the Second Hijri Century (c. 800 CE), during a time of unprecedented piety, trustworthiness and morality. Each Islamic locality was blessed with pious Scholars/Sulaha and Baghdad in 'Iraq, was the seat of the *Khaleefh* and the centre of Islamic learning. Residing in this city was the outstanding Shaykh Abu 'Abdullah al-Andalusee ✿, the spiritual guide of over 12,000 *mureeds*. He was also one of the leading scholars and *'Aimma* of Iraq; he knew 30,000 Ahadeeth by heart and could recite the Glorious Qur'ān from memory in all seven dialects of *qirā'at*.

Once he departed on a journey with his followers amongst whom were the renown Shaykh Junaid Baghdadi ✿ and Shaykh Shiblee ✿ who takes up the incident, 'The journey was passing with great ease, tranquillity and safety when we arrived at a Christian locality. It was time for salāh, however we had been unable to find water beforehand. As our entourage meandered through town in search of a water-supply, we noticed to our shock and amazement, people (Christians, Jews and Zoroastrians) worshipping at alters and shrines. Towards the outskirts of town, we found a well from which ladies were drawing water. Coincidently, the gaze of Shaykh Abu Abdullah al-Andalusee ✿ fell upon a lady who was the most beautiful amongst the group and the one adorned in fine clothes and jewellery. Immediately, the Shaykh's eyes, face and body language became transformed...he proceeded to ask the surrounding ladies, 'Whose daughter is this?' They replied, 'She is the daughter of our Chief Priest.'

Shaykh Abu Abdullah ﷺ asked: 'Then why has her father humiliated her by ordaining such a mundane task for her? Could he not appoint a servant for her?'

Ladies: 'Of course he could, but her father is a very intelligent and far-sighted person, he does not wish her to be enamoured because of his wealth and standing. If her habits become spoilt, how will she be of service to her husband after nikah?'

After this conversation, our Shaykh ﷺ lowered his head and sat on that very spot for three consecutive days; he did not talk, eat, drink or move except to perform the five daily Salāh. A substantial following of students and associates were present but at a complete loss as to what had happened or what to do?

On the third day, Shaykh Shiblee ﷺ advanced and spoke, 'O Shaykh! All your followers are worried and perplexed at this silence of yours...say something, what is the matter?'

Shaykh Abu Abdullah ﷺ: 'My dear friends! For how long may I hide my condition from you. The lady that I observed yesterday; her love has so completely overpowered my senses and limbs that it is impossible for me to leave this locality.'

Shaykh Shiblee ﷺ: 'O our master! You are the Shaykh of Iraq, unparalleled in knowledge, excellences, renunciation and worship. The numbers of your *mureedeen* total over 12,000. For Allah's ﷻ sake do not disgrace us!'

Shaykh Abu Abdullah ﷺ: 'My friends! Mine and your fate has been decreed by Allah ﷻ. The garment of Sainthood has been snatched away from me and the signs of guidance have been lifted. (He thereafter began to sob)… 'O my people! Fate has been decreed, it is all beyond my control.'

Shaykh Shiblee ﷁ continues, 'We were grief-stricken upon hearing this tale and crying profusely, our Shaykh was also sobbing with us to the extent that the ground became wet. Helplessly we departed for Baghdad. Hearing of our impending arrival, people from all over flocked to greet our Shaykh. Noticing his absence and our tale of events, a huge hue and commotion took place. Innumerable *mureedeen* were unable to tolerate this calamitous news and immediately passed-away; whilst others pleaded to Allah ﷻ, 'O the Transformer of hearts! Guide our Shaykh and return him to his rank and position.'

Very soon all the *Khanqahs* closed down and we spent an entire year in this sorrow and separation.

After a year, some of us *mureedeen* decided to visit him to ascertain his whereabouts and condition. A small contingent departed; when we arrived in the non-Muslim locality we inquired from the locals who replied, 'He shepherds the pigs in the jungle.' Astonished, we asked, 'What has happened?'

Locals: 'He requested the Chief Priest to marry his daughter. He stipulated four conditions: the Shaykh should become a Christian; he would wear a crucifix; he would shepherd pigs and he would stand upon the Glorious Qur'ān.' He accepted the first three but refused the fourth. This is why you will find him in the jungle tending to the pigs.'

Shaykh Shiblee ﷁ: 'Our hearts palpated upon hearing this news; we sobbed openly; with great difficulty we proceeded towards the jungle in search of him. We observed him from afar, wearing a Christian hat and cross; tending to the pigs with the staff he used to lean against whilst delivering sermon (*khutbah*) upon Hadeeth. This was rubbing salt into the wound. When he observed us coming, he lowered his head. We arrived closer and offered *salāms*. Shaykh Abu 'Abdullah ﷺ replied in a very faint voice...

Shaykh Shiblee ﷺ: 'O Shaykh! In spite of such Uloom, excellences, Hadeeth and Tafseer, what is this condition of yours?'

Shaykh Abu 'Abdullah ﷺ: 'O my brothers! I have no choice. Whatever my Lord intended, He ﷻ has made me. After making me so close (*muqarrab*), He ﷻ has thrown me so far; who is able to alter His Decree? O Friends! Fear the Wrath and Anger of Allah ﷻ, the Independent. Do not become proud upon your knowledge and excellences.' Thereafter he raised his head towards the Heavens, 'O my Lord! I had not thought this possible about You, that You would humiliate and cast me away from Your Door!' He thereafter repented and cried...'*Independence of thou O Magnificent One, what has it not done to this poor and sinful one.*' O Shiblee! Fortunate is he who derives lesson and admonition from others!'

Shaykh Shiblee ﷺ (crying and barely able to speak, prayed to Allah ﷻ):

> '*O our Creator! It is your Help we seek and it is to You from Whom we seek Forgiveness. In all affairs we rely solely upon You. Remove this calamity from us for there is none besides You who may defer.*'

Hearing this crying and wailing, all the pigs gathered and began to bray and cry with such force that the surrounding valleys and mountains reverberated with their screams.

Shaykh Shiblee ﷺ: 'Shaykh, you were a Hāfiz of the Glorious Qur'ān and could recite it in any of the seven *qirā'ats*, do you still remember any portion of it?'

Shaykh Abu 'Abdullah ﷺ: 'O friend! I remember nothing of the Glorious Qur'ān except two verses. One Verse is,

'Whomsoever Allah ﷻ disgraces, none is able to grant him respect. Undoubtedly, Allah ﷻ enacts whatever He wishes.' (22:18)

And the second Verse is,

'Whomsoever has chosen kufr in-lieu of Imān, undoubtedly he has wavered from the Straight Path.' (2:108)

Shaykh Shiblee ﷺ: 'Shaykh, you memorised 30,000 hadeeth with the Chain of Narration (*sanad*), are you able to recall any from amongst them?'

Shaykh Abu Abdullah ﷺ: 'I remember only one Hadeeth!

'Whomsoever forgoes his Deen, execute him!'

Shaykh Shiblee ﷺ: 'Seeing this state of heartbreaking affairs we sorrowfully left our Shaykh there and departed towards Baghdad. We had reached three *manzils* by the third day, when suddenly we observed our Shaykh emerging from a river in-front of us reciting the *Kalimah Shahadah* loudly after having bathed (*ghusl*). Only that person would be able to comprehend our joy who had contemplated on our sorrow, predicament and grief.

Shaykh Abu Abdullah ﷺ: 'Bring for me a pure piece of cloth.'

Dressing he firstly prayed salāh. We waited patiently to hear. After praying, he turned towards us and sat down.

Shaykh Shiblee ﷺ: 'Thousands of thanks to Allah ﷻ who has joined us together and rekindled our *Jamā'at* after its tethers were broken. Inform us, how have you returned after this great calamity?'

Shaykh Abu Abdullah ﷺ: 'My friends! When you left me to return, I humbly pleaded and prayed, 'O Allah ﷻ! Deliver me from this calamity and imprisonment (*jinjal*) for I am Your sinful and errant servant.' That Accepter of Prayers listened to my plea and forgave all my sins.'

Shaykh Shiblee 🌸: 'Was there a reason for this calamity and trial?'

Shaykh Abu Abdullah 🌸: 'Yes! When we arrived at that village and observed those people praying at churches, alters and shrines to other deities besides Allah 🕮...pride and airs arose in my heart, that we are Believers whilst these wretches are fools and idiots in worshipping lifeless idols. At that time an unseen voice addressed me, 'This *Imān* and *tawheed* are not your personal excellences, all are bestowed through our *tawfeeq*. Why, do you consider your *Imān* to be a personal achievement? If you wish, We could immediately show you!' At that time I perceived something like a bird flying out from my heart; in reality it was my *Imān*.

Shaykh Shiblee 🌸: 'After this, our caravan returned to Baghdad, where all the *mureedeen* witnessing our Shaykh's return to the fold of Islam expressed their happiness. Even the *Caliph* came to meet and conferred gifts. The *Khanqah* reopened and our Shaykh returned to his original spiritual practices; he restudied Hadeeth and Tafseer from his scholarly associates and once again commenced delivering lectures, lessons, instructions and spiritual training of followers. He excelled and surpassed his previous expertise, competence and status, with the number of his students increasing to 40,000. This progress continued and one day as we were sitting in his company a knock was suddenly heard; I walked over to find a saintly person dressed in black clothes standing. I asked who he was, where he had come from and why?'

Visitor: 'Inform your Shaykh, the lady whom you left behind in the village wishes to become a *Muslimah* and stay in the company of the pious.'

> *'Whosoever becomes Allah's 🕮, the entire creation becomes his;*
>
> *And whosoever forsakes Allah 🕮 then all creation gives him amiss.'*

Shaykh Shiblee 🌸: 'I returned to my Shaykh and related what had transpired. Immediately the Shaykh's face turned red and he began to tremble out of fear. Thereafter, he granted the lady permission to enter. Instantly upon observing our Shaykh, the lady began to weep so frantically that she was unable to speak.

Shaykh Abu Abdullah ﷺ (addressing her): 'How and why did you come here?'

Lady ﷺ: 'O Shaykh! Since you had left our village and I was informed of your departure, I have been in such a state of restlessness and turmoil which only my heart is aware; no hunger or thirst. Sleep was out of the question. It was in this state of agitation that towards dawn I laid down for a while and whilst in this state of slumber I observed a vision wherein a person was addressing me, 'If you wish to become a *Muminah* then forsake idol worship and follow your Shaykh. Repent and forgo your creed and enter the religion of the Shaykh.' In the dream I asked, 'What is the Shaykh's religion?'

Person: 'His religion is Islam.'

Lady ﷺ: 'What is Islam?'

Person: 'To firmly accept verbally and with one's heart that there is no God besides Allah ﷻ and Prophet Muhammad ﷺ is His true Messenger.'

Lady ﷺ: 'How may I follow and reach the Shaykh?'

Person: 'Close you eyes and hold onto this rope.'

Lady ﷺ: 'Very well,' as I closed my eyes and grabbed the rope. After a short while and having taken a few steps, I was ordered to open my eyes and I found myself in Baghdad on the banks of the River Tigris, astonished as to how I could have possibly arrived here in seconds.'

Person (pointing towards the *Khanqah*): 'This is the Shaykh's residence, you go there and tell him his brother Al-Khidr ﷺ sends *salāms*.'